Sustainable Finance and Impact Investing

Sustainable Finance and Impact Investing

Alan S. Gutterman

BEP

BUSINESS EXPERT PRESS

Leader in applied, concise business books

Sustainable Finance and Impact Investing

Copyright © Business Expert Press, LLC, 2021.

Cover design by Charlene Kronstedt

Interior design by Exeter Premedia Services Private Ltd., Chennai, India

First published in 2021 by
Business Expert Press, LLC
222 East 46th Street, New York, NY 10017
www.businessexpertpress.com

ISBN-13: 978-1-63742-002-7 (paperback)
ISBN-13: 978-1-63742-003-4 (e-book)

Business Expert Press Finance and Financial Management Collection

Collection ISSN: 2331-0049 (print)
Collection ISSN: 2331-0057 (electronic)

First edition: 2021

10 9 8 7 6 5 4 3 2 1

Description

The term impact investing first appeared in 2008. Today the most commonly used definition is investing made with the intention to generate positive, measurable social and environmental impact alongside a financial return. A wide range of individual and institutional investors that have already entered the impact investment marketplace and continued growing enthusiasm can be expected given that feedback from investors indicated that portfolio performance has generally met or exceed their expectations for both social and environmental impact and financial return.

Established companies have been compelled to respond to calls by institutional investors to incorporate responsible environmental, social, and governance initiatives into their business models as a condition to continued support in public capital markets. Other companies seeking to demonstrate to impact investors their commitment to environmental and social responsibility have opted for emerging forms of legal entities, so-called social enterprises, which explicitly incorporate sustainability and multi-stakeholder interests into their governance and reporting frameworks.

This book provides readers with a basic understanding of sustainable finance and impact investing including history, definitions of impact, current trends and drivers, future challenges, and an overview of the key players in the global impact ecosystem. The book also describes impact investment structures and instruments, social enterprises, and impact measurement and reporting.

Keywords

impact investment; impact; environmental performance; social performance; sustainable development; integrated reporting; venture capital; private equity

Contents

CHAPTER 1

Sustainable Finance

In recent years governments have debated and established ambitious public policy initiatives such as the 2030 Agenda for Sustainable Development and its broad range of Sustainable Development Goals (SDGs) including reducing poverty worldwide and promoting sustainable economic growth and the Paris climate agreement of 2015. Funding these initiatives would require the deployment of massive amounts of external financing, much of which would need to come from governments in the form of "official development assistance," which has been defined as government aid that promotes and specifically targets the economic development and welfare of developing countries. Multilateral development banks (MDBs), which are created by governments including the World Bank and International Monetary Fund, also play a significant role in stimulating and channeling aid into developed, low-income and emerging companies. Other significant forms of external financing assistance in the development sector include philanthropic assistance through foundations, international sovereign bond issuance across various multilateral institutions including MDBs, development institutions and supranational organizations, and climate finance through public–private partnerships. Capital for development projects is also being provided by financial institutions, insurance funds, pension funds, and impact investors, and organizations active in the startup community are ramping up their support for sustainable entrepreneurship. More and more companies are issuing financing instruments based on specific promises of use of the funds for environmental and/or social projects and stock exchanges are facilitating these offerings by mandating more robust environmental, social, and governance disclosures. The actions of all of these actors are influenced by the priorities identified by nonprofit think tanks, philanthropists, social change activists, and enablers and civil society.[1]

Sustainable finance has been explained to be a long-term approach to finance and investing, emphasizing long-term thinking, decision-making and value creation, and has also been described as the interrelationships that exist between environmental, social, and governance (ESG) issues on the one hand, and financing, lending, and investment decisions, on the other and long-term-oriented financial decision-making that integrates ESG considerations.[2] On its webpage describing "sustainable finance," the European Commission (EC) explained that the term generally referred to the process of taking due account of environmental and social considerations when making investment decisions, leading to increased investment in longer-term and sustainable activities. Examples of environmental considerations offered by the EC included climate change mitigation and adaptation, as well as the environment more broadly and the related risks (e.g., natural disasters), while social considerations refer to issues such as inequality, inclusiveness, labor relations, investment in human capital, and communities. The EC also noted that the governance of public and private institutions, including their management structures, employee relations, and executive remuneration practices, played a fundamental role in ensuring the inclusion of social and environmental considerations in the decision-making process. The EC's view was that all of the components of ESG were integral parts of sustainable economic development and finance, and that sustainable finance should be understood as

---

[1] The discussion in this paragraph is adapted from Sustainable Finance (The Middle Road), https://themiddleroad.org/sustainable-finance-unleashed/

[2] Krauss, A., P. Kruger, and J. Meyer. September 2016. *Sustainable Finance in Switzerland: Where Do We Stand?* Zurich: Sustainable Finance Institute, 13 and 15. According to the CFA Institute, examples of environmental issues include climate change and carbon emissions, air and water pollution, biodiversity, deforestation, energy efficiency, waste management, and water scarcity; examples of social factors include customer satisfaction, data protection, and privacy, gender and diversity, employee engagement, community relations, human rights, and labor standards and examples of governance factors include board composition, audit committee structure, bribery and corruption, executive compensation, lobbying, political contributions, and whistleblower schemes. Id. at 16.

financing that can support economic growth and the reduction of pressures on the environment while simultaneously taking into account social and governance aspects.[3]

Sustainable finance has emerged in parallel to policy initiatives mentioned above as it has become clear that they cannot be realistically undertaken and completed without innovative private sector financing models that allow a wide range of potential investors to participate in high-growth, albeit risky and uncertain, opportunities. According to BNP Paribas, capital for sustainable finance is available from investors who want to take part in financing enterprises involved in projects with high environmental or social value, including projects that will have an impact that the investors may experience directly; socially responsible investment funds capitalized by institutional and private investors; pension funds and private banking and wealth management sources expected to grow significantly in the coming decades due to wealth transfers from Baby Boomers and Generation X to Millennials who surveys indicate have a strong commitment to incorporate social change into their investment decisions.[4] Sustainable finance is just not about "doing good," in fact consultants such as McKinsey have argued that companies with a robust ESG framework are more likely to add value as compared to companies that have not developed sustainable practices and that ESG creates value in several different ways including top-line growth, cost reductions, reduced regulatory and legal interventions, employee productivity uplift, and investment and asset optimization as key enablers in generating a long-term advantage.[5]

The interest of the EC in sustainable finance has been driven by the European Green Deal, which is a growth strategy announced in December 2019 that seeks to make Europe the first climate-neutral continent by 2050. The EC has acknowledged that the scale of the investments

---

[3] https://ec.europa.eu/info/business-economy-euro/banking-and-finance/sustainable-finance/what-sustainable-finance_en

[4] https://group.bnpparibas/en/news/sustainable-finance-about

[5] Sustainable Finance (The Middle Road), https://themiddleroad.org/sustainable-finance-unleashed/ (citing Five Ways that ESG Creates Value, *McKinsey Quarterly*, November 14, 2019).

necessary to achieve the desired transition to a climate-neutral, green, competitive and inclusive economy is beyond the capacity of the public sector alone (e.g., in January 2020, the EC presented its European Green Deal Investment Plan that called for the mobilization of at least €1 trillion of sustainable investments through the period ending in 2030) and has committed to an action plan on sustainable finance in which the financial sector (e.g., asset managers, insurance companies, and investment or insurance advisors) supports the European Green Deal by reorienting investments toward more sustainable technologies and businesses; financing growth in a sustainable manner over the long term; and contributing to the creation of a low-carbon, climate resilient, and circular economy.[6]

The financial services industry has taken notice of importance of sustainable finance and the market for sustainable investment opportunities has been growing steadily as more and more industry participants are recognizing the long-term benefits of a more sustainable economy and incorporating sustainability considerations into their strategies and operations. According to data from the Global Sustainable Investment Alliance (GSIA), global sustainable investment assets reached $30.6 trillion at the start of 2018, a 34 percent increase from 2016, and the volume of global sustainable investment assets as a percentage of all assets under management around the world increased from 28 to 35 percent over that same period.[7] Reports based on data collected by the GSIA noted that the number of signatories to the Principles for Responsible Investing (PRI) had grown to 2,450 by June 2019, compared to 63 signatories at the time that the PRI was launched in 2006, and that aggregate assets under management for the group was $82 trillion. In October 2019

---

[6] https://ec.europa.eu/info/business-economy-euro/banking-and-finance/sustainable-finance/what-sustainable-finance_en

[7] 2018 Global Sustainable Investment Review (Global Sustainable Investment Alliance) (as reported in Changing Dynamics of Sustainable Finance: The regulatory push in the direction of sustainable growth, Sia Partners (February 25, 2020), https://sia-partners.com/en/news-and-publications/from-our-experts/changing-dynamics-sustainable-finance-regulatory-push) See also CNBC, Your complete guide to investing with a conscience, a $30 trillion market just getting started (December 14, 2019), https://cnbc.com/2019/12/14/your-complete-guide-to-socially-responsible-investing.html

the International Monetary Fund reported that ESG funds accounted for around $850 billion in assets. While early adoption of ESG factors among funds has been primarily on the equity side there have been indications that fixed income investors are becoming more comfortable with the concept as demonstrated by the growing rate of issuance of sustainability-linked bonds ("green bonds").[8]

Principles for Responsible Investment

The six UN Principles for Responsible Investment ("Principles") (unpri.org) are a voluntary and aspirational set of investment principles that offer a menu of possible actions for incorporating ESG issues into investment practice. The Principles were developed by an international group of institutional investors, for investors, through a process convened by the UN Secretary-General, and signatories are required under the Principles to make the following commitment:

"As institutional investors, we have a duty to act in the best long-term interests of our beneficiaries. In this fiduciary role, we believe that environmental, social, and corporate governance (ESG) issues can affect the performance of investment portfolios (to varying degrees across companies, sectors, regions, asset classes and through time). We also recognize that applying these Principles may better align investors with broader objectives of society. Therefore, where consistent with our fiduciary responsibilities, we commit to the following:

Principle 1: We will incorporate ESG issues into investment analysis and decision-making processes.

Principle 2: We will be active owners and incorporate ESG issues into our ownership policies and practices.

---

[8] Sia Partners. 2020. "Changing Dynamics of Sustainable Finance: The Regulatory Push in the Direction of Sustainable Growth." February 25, 2020, https://sia-partners.com/en/news-and-publications/from-our-experts/changing-dynamics-sustainable-finance-regulatory-push

Principle 3: We will seek appropriate disclosure on ESG issues by the entities in which we invest.

Principle 4: We will promote acceptance and implementation of the Principles within the investment industry.

Principle 5: We will work together to enhance our effectiveness in implementing the Principles.

Principle 6: We will each report on our activities and progress towards implementing the Principles."

The Principles include a menu of possible actions for incorporating ESG issues for each of the six Principles listed above. For example, with respect to "active ownership" (Principle 2), investors are asked to consider developing and disclosing an active ownership policy consistent with the Principles; exercising voting rights or monitoring compliance with voting policy (if outsourced); developing an engagement capability (either directly or through outsourcing); participating in the development of policy, regulation, and standard setting (such as promoting and protecting shareholder rights); filing shareholder resolutions consistent with long-term ESG considerations; engaging with companies on ESG issues; participating in collaborative engagement initiatives and asking investment managers to undertake and report on ESG-related engagement.

Source: https://unpri.org/pri/an-introduction-to-responsible-investment/what-are-the-principles-for-responsible-investment

Consistent with its leadership in other areas of sustainability and corporate social responsibility, Europe had the largest pool of sustainable investment assets globally as of 2018 and commentators have noted that sustainable investing has been broadly adopted in Europe and has reached the highest level of maturity compared to any other region. The United States trails slightly behind Europe and data indicates that Asia is progressively catching up and that sustainable investing is gaining more traction in Asian countries outside of Japan, which was one of the earliest adopters of ESG-based investing. China has been particularly aggressive—it had the second biggest green bond market in the world as of the end of 2018—and Australia, Hong Kong, and Singapore have launched initiatives to promote sustainable investing.[9]

At the same time, there has been a surge in regulatory focus on sustainable finance and developing approaches to integrating sustainable finance into the mainstream frameworks of governments, multinational enterprises, and the global financial services industry. For example, in May 2018 the EC released its Sustainable Finance Package, a set of legislative proposals focusing on driving more capital toward sustainable investment projects and encouraging participants in the financial sector to change their operations so as to reduce environmental risks. Key features of the package included adoption of an EU-wide classification system for sustainable investments and "environmentally sustainable economic activity," requiring asset managers and institutional investors to demonstrate how their investments are aligned with ESG objectives and disclose how they comply with their duties and creation of a new category of benchmarks of standard indices and standardization of formatting for reporting of ESG disclosures. In Asia, stock exchanges in China and Hong Kong have mandated disclosures of ESG matters by their listed companies and countries such as China and India have begun to require that asset managers must incorporate ESG methodologies, strategies, and benchmarks into their investment decisions as opposed to the voluntary guidelines that have applied in the past.[10]

BNP Paribas noted that businesses have a key role to play in the evolution and growth of sustainable finance by embracing ESG-focused financing instruments and related practices such as more robust disclosures of their ESG performance. For example, Apple has issued green bonds to finance energy efficiency projects and Starbucks used a sustainable bond to raise $500 million to underwrite ethical coffee production.[11] Between September 2016 and June 2020, Mitsubishi UFG Financial Group issued seven Green Bonds, one Social Bond, and one Sustainability Bond for a total amount of $3.2 billion equivalent, and noted that the net proceeds from the Green Bonds were allocated to projects that

---

[9] Id. See also Sustainable Finance (The Middle Road), https://themiddleroad.org/sustainable-finance-unleashed/
[10] Id.
[11] https://group.bnpparibas/en/news/sustainable-finance-about

address environmental issues, such as renewable energy or energy efficiency projects, the proceeds from Social Bonds were allocated to projects that tackle important social issues such as affordable housing, health, and education and the proceeds from Sustainability Bonds were allocated to a combination of both environmental and social projects.[12] Verizon's $1 billion green bond offering in February 2019 was the first by an American telecom company. It was way oversubscribed and the proceeds were earmarked for projects in renewable energy, energy efficiency, green buildings, sustainable water management, and biodiversity and conservation.[13]

A great deal of analysis has been undertaken in order to support the business case for sustainable finance by demonstrating risk-adjusted outperformance of sustainable investments and, in fact, the Swiss Finance Institute (SFI) cited a comprehensive analysis released in 2015 that covered the results of more than 2,000 academic studies on the link between ESG questions and found that the overwhelming number of the studies identified a significantly neutral or positive correlation between ESG and financial performance at the level of the firm.[14] However, the SFI went

---

[12] https://mufg.jp/english/ir/fixed_income/greenbond/index.html

[13] https://greenbiz.com/article/investors-scrambled-get-verizons-1b-green-bond-deal

[14] Krauss, A., P. Kruger, and J. Meyer. September 2016. *Sustainable Finance in Switzerland: Where Do We Stand?* Zurich: Swiss Finance Institute, 21 (citing Friede, G., T. Busch, and A. Bassen. 2015. "ESG and Financial Performance: Aggregated Evidence From More Than 2,000 Empirical Studies." *Journal of Sustainable Finance and Investment* 5, no. 4, p. 210). See also Clark, G., A. Feiner, and M. Viehs. March 2015. "From the Stockholder to the Stakeholder: How Sustainability Can Drive Financial Outperformance." Working Paper and Wang, Q., J. Dou, and S. Jia. 2015. "A Meta-Analytic Review of Corporate Social Responsibility and Corporate Financial Performance: The Moderating Effect of Contextual Factors." *Business & Society* 27, no. 3, p. 1. The SFI cautioned that different types of sustainable investment come with varying levels of risk and return: ". . . thematic investments, which are often concentrated industry bets, are fundamentally different from screening approaches, ESG integration, or impact investing. A very strict exclusionary strategy could lead to a dramatically smaller investment universe that inhibits efficient risk diversification and might reduce investment performance. At the same time, the exclusion of certain unsustainable securities might have a positive impact on financial performance due to the better management of ESG risks or to the identification of mispriced assets." Id.

on to argue that "sustainable finance ought to play a prominent role in financial markets even in the absence of risk-adjusted outperformance" given that the financial sector plays an important and pivotal role in the future structure of the economy through the decision it makes in allocating capital to projects that contribute to sustainable development (e.g., energy efficiency, pollution reduction, humane work conditions, and reduced biodiversity loss).[15] According to the SFI's assessment of future priorities for participants in the Swiss financial system, "business as usual is no longer a valid option for most players, at least in the medium to long term" and financial institutions and regulators will need to pay attention to anticipated high demand for sustainable finance products driven by factors such as generational differences in preferences and changing societal expectations for finance.[16]

Sustainable finance has made significant progress and the percentage of assets that were professionally managed according to sustainability principles increased steadily over the first fifteen years of the twenty-first century, reaching about 30 percent as of 2015; however, a report prepared by the Global Sustainable Investment Alliance in that year declared that sustainable finance had not yet reached the core and mainstream of financial markets.[17] There are several key issues and challenges that need to be addressed and overcome for the sector to continue to grow to the point where it can play the desired role in pursuit and achievement of SDGs and other environmental and social public policy initiatives. For example, many companies have been accused of "ESG washing" and while steps are being taken to create more rigorous and standardized measures of ESG criteria there is still much work to be done. There has also been concern that the focus on ESG has been driven primarily by a search for new forms of financial gain as opposed to a serious interest in environmental and social innovation and impact. In addition, although there is a movement to standardize the terms and conditions of financial instruments

---

[15] Id.

[16] Id. at 43.

[17] Krauss, A., P. Kruger, and J. Meyer. September 2016. *Sustainable Finance in Switzerland: Where Do We Stand?*. Zurich: Swiss Finance Institute, 13 (citing Global Sustainable Investment Review 2014. February 2015. Global Sustainable Investment Alliance).

such as sustainable bonds and achieve a consensus on descriptors of impact and measurement tools, sustainable finance projects are necessarily complex and carry significant legal and other expenses that make it difficult to fund projects that are unlikely to scale. Additional work is needed to improve liquidity for sustainable financing instruments, a process that will require collaboration among stock exchanges, investment banks and multinational institutions. Also required by investors, as well as governments and other actors in the sustainable finance sector, is a robust and universally accepted framework of quantitative and qualitative benchmarks for measuring and reporting sustainable development performance.

Increasing attention is being placed on the roles of banks and other financial institutions in the transition toward a sustainable global economy. The SFI argued about the need to overcome several perceived barriers to more widespread adoption of sustainable financing among banks and other financial institutions including the complexity of the issue, knowledge gaps at all levels, cultural and generational conflicts, misconceptions about sustainable finance, a lack of standardization and terminology, and the difficulties associated with keeping up with the fast pace of product and policy innovation in the field.[18] KPMG advised banks to take steps to understand the common ESG expectations of their key stakeholders and build awareness of leading ESG practices among senior management and board members; acquire and/or develop the right capabilities and process to monitor and manage ESG appropriately; dialogue with regulatory authorities to understand what will be expected of banks with respect to ESG and proactively participate in development of standards; integrate ESG factors into their existing assessments of credit and valuation risks in their portfolios; and develop an actionable and measureable strategy for addressing and mitigating ESG risks.[19]

---

[18] Id. at 10.

[19] Embedding ESG into banks strategies: Four key actions banks should be taking to prepare for the post-COVID-19 ESG mantra (KPMG, May 2020), https://home.kpmg/xx/en/home/insights/2020/05/embedding-esg-into-banks-strategies.html

Sustainable Investment Strategies

Sustainable investing was originally based on negative/exclusionary or screen approaches that excluded individual assets or sectors from consideration for inclusion in a portfolio based on moral or ethical considerations. While it has been estimated that negative/exclusionary screening continues to represent the largest category of sustainable investment,[20] the market has gradually expanded to include additional categories based on classifications developed and used by organizations such as the CFA Institute and the Global Sustainable Investment Alliance (GSIA)[21]:

- *Negative/exclusionary screening*: Negative or exclusionary screening consists of avoiding specific assets due to consideration of specific ESG criteria including moral values (e.g., tobacco or gambling), standards and norms (e.g., human rights), ethical convictions (e.g., animal testing), or legal requirements (e.g., controversial armaments such as cluster bombs or land mines, excluded in order to comply with international conventions).[22] Companies engaged in "negative" sectors, activities, or practices must be prepared to make significant modifications to their business models in

---

[20] It has been estimated that, as of 2016 at least, that negative/exclusionary screening represented the largest category of sustainable investment: about two-thirds. See The Economist Explains: What Is Sustainable Finance?" The Economist, April 17, 2018, https://economist.com/the-economist-explains/2018/04/17/what-is-sustainable-finance

[21] Krauss, A., P. Kruger, and J. Meyer. September 2016. *Sustainable Finance in Switzerland: Where Do We Stand?* Zurich: Sustainable Finance Institute, 18–19; Environmental, Social and Governance Issues in Investing: A Guide for Investment Professionals (CFA Institute, 2015); and Changing Dynamics of Sustainable Finance: The regulatory push in the direction of sustainable growth, Sia Partners (February 25, 2020), https://sia-partners.com/en/news-and-publications/from-our-experts/changing-dynamics-sustainable-finance-regulatory-push

[22] For an example of a comprehensive statement of minimum standards and exclusions applicable to an impact investment program, see Triodos Minimum Standards and Exclusions, https://triodos.com/downloads/about-triodos-bank/triodos-banks-minimum-standards.pdf

order access capital from investors and lenders applying these types of screens.

- *Best-in-class/positive screening*: "Best-in-class" (positive) screening contrasts significantly with negative screening and calls for investment and lending decisions to be made based on demonstrated high ESG performance of sectors, companies, or projects. Investors can rely on a growing number of reference indexes to select projects that can improve both the risk and return aspects of their portfolio and companies need to be mindful of the criteria applied by the reference indexes and track their performance, although it should be understood that such indexes are not infallible and that it remains difficult to reliably measure ESG performance.

- *Norm-based screening*: Norm-based screening involves screening potential investments against minimum standards of business practice based on international norms relating to climate protection, human rights, working conditions, and action plans against corruption.

- *ESG integration*: ESG integration involves new and emerging methodologies intended to systematically and explicitly include ESG risks and opportunities into traditional financial-based investment analysis. ESG integration differs from ESG indexing mentioned above in that it does not rely on benchmarking ESG performance vis-à-vis peers. As with ESG indexing, companies need to understand the how investment analysis taking ESG risks and opportunities into consideration is conducted, not only to gain a better understanding of the expectations of investors but also to potentially improve their own risk-adjusted rate of return on assets and mitigate sustainability-related risks. ESG integration has become the second largest category of sustainable investment following negative/exclusionary screening.

- *Impact investing*: Impact investing is aimed directly at creating a positive environmental or social impact by identifying and solving a particular environmental or social problem and has been described as "investments made in companies, organizations, and funds with the intention of generating social and environmental impact (pursuit of positive externalities) alongside a financial return." So far, impacting investing, which has often focused on microfinance and development investing for the benefit of underserved individuals or communities, has been available mostly through private markets from funds managed by specialized asset managers. Investment philosophies of impact investors range from market-driven risk-adjusted returns to concessional and capital preservation. Access to capital from impact investors may be limited for companies that lack scalable high-quality investment projects.

- *Thematic investments*: Thematic investments include investment activities focused on specific high-profile sustainability-related themes such as cleantech, infrastructure, energy-efficient real estate or sustainable forestry. Thematic investments are projected to become increasing important for certain long-term oriented investors such as pension funds, insurance companies and sovereign wealth funds.

- *Active ownership*: Active ownership, sometimes referred to as "corporate engagement and shareholder action," takes a different approach to sustainable finance by focusing on engagement and dialogue with portfolio companies after an initial investment is made in order to influence ESG strategies and actions through exercise of ownership rights and being a visible activist for change. The growing role of activism can be seen by charting the increasing numbers of proxy votes relating to ESG issues, a trend that has materially impacted how boards and senior executives manage investor relations.

A difference lens on the landscape of investors interested in providing financing to companies engaged in the pursuit of business models that contribute to sustainable development was offered by BNP Paribas (BNP)[23]:

- *Socially Responsible Investing* (SRI): SRI is the most widely understood approach to sustainable finance and involves integrating ESG criteria, in a systematic and traceable manner, into decisions on financial management and investment and encouraging asset managers to consider extra-financial criteria when selecting asset values.
- *Green Finance*: Often viewed as a subset of SRI, green finance includes all transactions that are addressed toward energy transition and combating climate change. Green finance is often executed by the issuance of green bonds and the growing popularity of those instruments has led to global investors to take steps toward standardizing terms in order to make the capital raising process more efficient. Asset managers may also contribute by decarbonizing their portfolios in order to limit their ecological footprint.
- *Social Impact Investing*: Social impact investing, or social finance, includes investments into projects that have a social focus and seek to address a particular social or environmental challenge. Sometimes referred to as solidarity-based finance, investments in this area typically target unemployment, housing problems caused by increased poverty, environmental issues such as organic farming or clean energy and development of third world economies.[24]
- *Social Business*: Social businesses were described by BNP as being primarily social in nature but following viable economic models—in other words, a shared value concept that seeks both profit and social impact. With the consent of investors, profits are reinvested to combat exclusion, protect the

---

[23] https://group.bnpparibas/en/news/sustainable-finance-about

[24] For further information on social impact investing, see the website of Finansol (https://finansol.org/en/index.php), a French organization that certifies certain social finance products and monitors trends in social finance.

environment, or promote development and solidarity. Forms of social business include microfinance, impact investing, and Social Impact Bonds (i.e., bonds that are repaid upon maturation only if the social objectives of the project have been achieved).

Banks and Other Commercial Financing Institutions

Banks and other financial institutions become subject to environmental and social risks when they provide financial services to companies that are associated with illegal activities or controversial issues (e.g., hydraulic fracturing, arctic drilling, palm oil, soy, or coal-fired power plants), including business practices, sectors, projects, and/or countries that are directly or indirectly, or allegedly or actually, associated with detrimental environmental and social impacts.[25] In order to act responsibly in relation to these risks, financial institutions need to implement a framework for conducting credit and operational risk assessments that integrate consideration of environmental and social issues and measures of ESG performance and risk. Financial institutions are referring to measures from credit agencies that are beginning to integrate ESG into their assessments; however, many have criticized the accuracy and utility of these ratings. Financial institutions are also conducting their own due diligence based on the Equator Principles, a risk management framework that was adopted in 2013 and originally developed to support financial institutions in determining, assessing, and managing the environmental and social risks related to project financing. In addition, given that all companies, including financial institutions, are subject to heightened scrutiny relating to their involvement with activities that have adverse human rights impacts, banks, and other financial institutions are voluntary adopting and implementing the human rights due diligence standards and protocols called for by the UN Guiding Principles on Business and Human Rights and the OECD Guidelines for Multinational

---

[25] Krauss, A., P. Kruger, and J. Meyer. September 2016. *Sustainable Finance in Switzerland: Where Do We Stand?* Zurich: Swiss Finance Institute, 20.

Enterprises.[26] The various voluntary standards referred to above are likely to be supplemented by adoption of some form of sustainability-focused banking regulations given the potential broad adverse impacts of material environmental and social risks to the stability of individual banks and the financial system as a whole.[27]

KPMG argued that ESG, particularly concerns about climate change, will become an increasingly important influence in the global economy in the wake of the COVID-19 pandemic and that banks and financial institutions will face increasing pressures from various stakeholders to embed ESG into their strategies. For example, KPMG predicted that regulators, oversight authorities, and policymakers would become more vocal about the need for greater adoption of ESG and that investors would show stronger interest in ESG-related projects and funds, particularly since data from the first quarter of 2020 provided evidence that 70 percent of responsible investment funds outperformed their peers and that the MSCI World ESG Leaders Index outperformed the regular index by 1.36 percent in that quarter. KPMG also noted that banks, like other businesses, would be feeling growing pressure from customers and the public at large to act in a manner that reflects their views and beliefs regarding environmental and social responsibility, and that consumers, particularly those in younger generations, would choose their banks based on their ESG credentials.[28]

According to a global survey conducted by KPMG International in 2019, before the COVID-19 pandemic, almost three-quarters of bank

[26] Id. (citing UN Guiding Principles on Business and Human Rights, Discussion Paper for Banks on Implications of Principles (Thun Group of Banks, 2015), 16–21).

[27] Id. (citing Policy Briefing: Financial Stability and Environmental Stability (Cambridge Institute for Sustainability Leadership and United Nations Environment Programme, September 2015) and The Financial System We Need: Aligning the Financial System with Sustainable Development (UN Environment Programme, 2015)).

[28] Embedding ESG into banks strategies: Four key actions banks should be taking to prepare for the post-COVID-19 ESG mantra (KPMG, May 2020), https://home.kpmg/xx/en/home/insights/2020/05/embedding-esg-into-banks-strategies.html

CEOs acknowledged that the future growth of their institutions would be largely determined by their ability to successfully navigate the transition to a low-carbon, clean-technology economy.[29] However, banks and industry policymakers recognize that in order for this to occur, there needs to be a coordinated and collaborative response from all parts of the banking industry and the broader financial system. There is some movement in this direction, such as the Principles for Responsible Banking launched in November 2018 and embraced by a third of the world's largest banks, discussions involving banks and regulators relating to taxonomy and green finance and the creation of the Network for Greening the Financial System (www.ngfs.net), which is a group of central banks and supervisors willing, on a voluntary basis, to share best practices and contribute to the development of environment and climate risk management in the financial sector and to mobilize mainstream finance to support the transition toward a sustainable economy.

The Principles for Responsible Banking (PRB) are part of the United Nations Environment Programme Finance Initiative (UNEP FI), a partnership between the United Nations Environment Programme and global financial sector to mobilize private sector finance for sustainable development. UNEP FI works with more than 300 members—banks, insurers, and investors—and over 100 supporting institutions—to help create a financial sector that serves people and planet while delivering positive impacts and supports global finance sector principles, such as the PRB, to catalyze integration of sustainability into financial market practice. The goal of the PRB was to create a unique framework for ensuring that signatory banks' strategy and practice aligned with the vision society has set out for its future in the SDGs and the Paris Climate Agreement. The PRB that signatory banks commit to are[30]:

1. *Alignment*: We will align our business strategy to be consistent with and contribute to individuals' needs and society's goals, as expressed in the Sustainable Development Goals, the Paris Climate Agreement, and relevant national and regional frameworks.

---

[29] Id.

[30] https://unepfi.org/banking/bankingprinciples/

2. *Impact*: We will continuously increase our positive impacts while reducing the negative impacts on, and managing the risks to, people and environment resulting from our activities, products, and services. To this end, we will set and publish targets where we can have the most significant impacts.

3. *Clients and customers*: We will work responsibly with our clients and our customers to encourage sustainable practices and enable economic activities that create shared prosperity for current and future generations.

4. *Stakeholders*: We will proactively and responsibly consult, engage, and partner with relevant stakeholders to achieve society's goals.

5. *Governance and target setting*: We will implement our commitment to these Principles through effective governance and a culture of responsible banking.

6. *Transparency and accountability*: We will periodically review our individual and collective implementation of these principles and be transparent about and accountable for our positive and negative impacts and our contribution to society's goals.

As of July 2020, more than 170 banks had become signatories to the PRB and thus committed not only to adhere to the principles outlined above but also to continuously analyze their current impact on people and planet; based on this analysis, set targets where they have the most significant impact, and implement them; and publicly report on progress. Signatory banks must meet all of these requirements within four years of signing; however, with eighteen months of signature banks must begin reporting on their impact, how they are implementing the PRB, the targets they have set and the progress they have made.

Each bank needs to consider how to handle so-called transition risks (i.e., the risk associated with transitioning a bank's portfolio away from "brown" assets to greener and more sustainable investments). For example, brown assets continue to be profitable for many banks and any decision to reduce investments in those assets must take into account fiduciary duties to shareholders. At the same time, reducing financing to businesses operating based on brown assets, such as coal mines, will improve a bank's ESG-related disclosures but may also create unintended adverse consequences such as disruptions in communities if jobs are lost due to closures of businesses denied bank financing (which would also have an adverse impact on the bank's retail lending in the community).

In spite of the challenges, large global banks such as Goldman Sachs and the Bank of America have announced significant commitments of capital and other resources to greener finance, often doing so in a way that makes it clear that the issues and opportunities associated with ESG have been elevated to the CEO-level and the boardroom. KPMG reported that new products and models are continuously being created, tested, and commercialized, noting specifically that wealth managers had been moving toward ESG-informed investing; retail banks were creating new sustainable banking and investing products and services, such as green home-improvement loans, carbon neutral banking, and a variety of ESG-linked funds such as sustainable exchange-traded funds (ETFs), aimed at millennials; capital markets were moving toward "green underwriting" and syndicates of commercial banks were collaborating on sustainability-linked financing transactions that offered borrowers lower rates if they achieved certain ESG-focused operational targets.[31]

Even before the COVID-19 pandemic, policymakers around the world were pushing for business and regulatory initiatives to expand the footprint of banks and other financial institutions in offering sustainable financing. In Switzerland, for example, the majority of the larger financial market players still regard sustainable finance as a niche/specialized area and adopt strategies in which traditional and sustainable finance products coexist, and only a few institutions have opted for a full integration of sustainable finance and proactively adopted it as their unique selling proposition.[32] The SFI has called for a credible commitment to, and stronger support for, sustainable finance from the upper echelons of the Swiss financial sector (i.e., board and executive level), recommending expanded sustainable finance-related education for senior management, board members, and (chief) executives; reducing investment barriers for pension funds and other institutional investors and an official endorsement

---

[31] Id.

[32] Krauss, A., P. Kruger, and J. Meyer. September 2016. *Sustainable Finance in Switzerland: Where Do We Stand?* Zurich: Swiss Finance Institute, 10.

of sustainability as a core principle of the Swiss financial marketplace and a priority for policymakers. The SFI has suggested that financial institutions prioritize sustainable finance education, training, and development at all hierarchical levels and build more in-house expertise on sustainability issues and approaches that is integrated throughout all core divisions (i.e., by integrating expert sustainability teams throughout the organization as opposed to compartmentalizing sustainable knowledge in a separate, often marginalized, team or group).[33]

Blended Finance

Blended finance has been widely touted as being critical to achievement of the target of SDGs by 2030 and as an innovative strategy to pool in commercial capital to aid risk-adjusted return for development projects. Blended finance offers private investors a "first loss guarantee" through the use of mezzanine or senior debt instruments, which provide them with priority over other actors in the development space (i.e., multilateral development banks, development finance institutions, foundations, governments, etc.) who make the initial investment in a project by taking subordinated debt or junior equity positions in the project and then seek to attract private and commercial investors to purchase senior debt by undertaking to cover their losses through guarantees, grants, and insurance. The initial investment is generally referred to as a "concessional investment" and is intended to provide capital and technical assistance to get the project up and running. Concessional investments are typically very high risk and offer below-market rates of return and the goal of such investments is to absorb a sufficient amount of the overall risk associated with the project to make it viable to investors who seek market-rate returns but will only do so when risks have been lowered and managed.

Brodsky noted that blended finance has the advantage of bringing capital to developed areas and to projects that would otherwise be overlooked by many investors wary of investing in lower-income markets and projects that are below investment grade and that blended finance also allows governments and development agencies to correct market

---

[33] Id. at 11 and 43–44.

failures without requiring them to finance development projects entirely with public funds. However, Brodsky cited an analysis of 117 blended finance deals that found that in only forty-three cases was more than half the funding for projects provided by private sources, suggesting that blended financing may not be leveraging as much private capital as is needed for long-term, sustainable investing. Moreover, the availability of a blended finance structure will not attract investors unless they can be convinced that the project can be scaled up and will ultimately achieve commercial viability and the anticipated social impact.[34] While blended finance appears to be a promising strategy that has attracted the attention of numerous big players in the financial sector, OECD data indicates that only $81 billion of blended finance was raised for development work during 2015–2019, with much of that capital being deployed for infrastructure and climate change in Africa and Asia.[35]

Sustainable Bonds

The first sustainable bond was launched in 2007 by the European Investment Bank and since then sustainable bonds have played a significant role in scaling up the financing of investments that provide environmental and social benefits and attracting private investors to supplement the funding available from governments to pursue the ambitious public policy initiatives mentioned above. Sustainable bonds are generally broken out into three categories—Green, Social, and Sustainability Bonds—and have been described as any type of bond instrument where the proceeds will

---

[34] Brodsky, S. 2019. "What Is Blended Finance?" *Impactivate* (September 5, 2019), https://theimpactivate.com/what-is-blended-finance/ There is a large library of readily available resources on blended finance including information and analysis from the World Economic Forum (https://weforum.org/reports/blended-finance-toolkit); OECD (http://oecd.org/development/financing-sustainable-development/blended-finance-principles/); Convergence (https://convergence.finance/); USAID (https://usaid.gov/cii/blended-finance), and ODI (https://odi.org/publications/11303-blended-finance-poorest-countries-need-better-approach)

[35] Sustainable Finance (The Middle Road), https://themiddleroad.org/sustainable-finance-unleashed/

be exclusively applied to eligible environmental and/or social projects. Their common trait is specifically targeting positive environmental and/or social impact. Also relevant are so-called Sustainability-Linked Bonds, which are any type of bond instrument for which the financial and/or structural characteristics can vary depending on whether the issuer achieves predefined Sustainability/ESG objectives.[36]

BBVA reported that the size of the global sustainability bond market as of June 30, 2019, was $584 billion, representing about 5 percent of a total global outstanding bond market estimated to be about $100 trillion, and that the percentage of sustainability bond issuances versus total bond issuances had continued to increase to an average of 2.6 percent in 2018 vs. 2 percent in 2017, despite a slight reduction in issuance of sustainability bonds in 2018 due to market volatility that impacted bond issuance globally.[37] Data from Environmental Finance's *Sustainable Bond Insights* showed the following levels of interest in various types of sustainable bonds in the first half of 2019 (with percentage change in each category over the first half of 2018): Green Bonds ($126 billion, increase of 35.7 percent), Social Bonds ($8.8 billion, increase of 63 percent), and Sustainability Bonds ($18.2 billion, increase of 98 percent). Green Bonds dominate issuance among sustainability bonds on a relative basis (approximately 83 percent); however, both Social and Sustainability Bonds increased their relative contributions to overall issuance from 2015 through 2018 and as of June 30, 2019, their percentages of the sustainability bond market stood at 6.3 and 10.6 percent respectively.[38]

As noted above, the first sustainable bond came out of Europe and European issuers have continued to dominate the market since then. According to BBVA, the relative sizes of the sustainability bond markets as of the end of 2018 in Europe, the United States, and China were $290 billion, $140 billion, and $90 billion, respectively. BBVA noted several important differences among these markets: Europe is highly

---

[36] https://icmagroup.org/green-social-and-sustainability-bonds/

[37] ESG Bond Market Key topics and trends for 2019 and beyond—getting the harmony right, BBVA (July 23, 2019), https://bbva.com/wp-content/uploads/2019/07/Green-Bonds-Getting-the-harmony-right.pdf

[38] Id.

diversified with banks contributing 21 percent of total sustainability bond issuance in 2018 and no other single sector contributing more than 15 percent of total issuance and legislative efforts are afoot to develop EU taxonomy and harmonize standards across the EU; the US market is largely self-regulated and much less diversified than in Europe (91 percent of 2018 sustainability bond issuance was from banks, supranationals, utilities, and real estate); in China banks contributed 72 percent of total sustainability bond issuance in 2018 and efforts have been made by the People's Bank of China to harmonize green bonds by issuing green bond certification guidelines.[39]

Green Bonds

Green Bonds have been described as including any type of bond instrument where the proceeds will be exclusively applied to finance or refinance, in part or in full, new, and/or existing eligible green projects (e.g., funding new and existing mortgages for energy-efficient residential buildings in Norway).[40] As the data referred to above indicates, Green Bonds is by far the largest segment among the various sustainability bonds and target projects relating to a number of themes included in the SDGs such as climate mitigation involved in the reduction of carbon; clean water and sanitation (SDG6); affordable and clean energy (SDG7); buildings and transport (SDG9); city infrastructure (e.g., low carbon buildings and transport (SDG11) and agriculture (SDG15). Although they are popular, some have expressed doubts about their impact. For example, in September 2020, *The Economist* reported on a study by the Bank for International Settlements of over 200 issuances of Green Bonds by larger companies from 2015 to 2018 and noted that the evidence appeared to be that the issuances did not seem to lead to de-carbonization and

---

[39] Id.

[40] https://icmagroup.org/green-social-and-sustainability-bonds/ and ESG Bond Market Key topics and trends for 2019 and beyond—getting the harmony right, BBVA (July 23, 2019), https://bbva.com/wp-content/uploads/2019/07/Green-Bonds-Getting-the-harmony-right.pdf

that the Green Bond marketplace did not significantly lower the cost of borrowing.[41]

The ICMA's Green Bond Principles: Voluntary Process Guidelines for Issuing Green Bonds (GBP) are intended to promote integrity in the Green Bond market through guidelines that recommend transparency, disclosure, and reporting. It is anticipated that setting the structure and terms of Green Bonds in alignment with the GBP will provide the underlying investment opportunity with transparent "green credentials" and that widespread adoption of the GBP will ultimately increase capital allocation to green projects. The ICMA has noted that the GBP are collaborative and consultative in nature based on the contributions of members and observers of the Green Bond Principles and Social Bond Principles, and of the wider community of stakeholders. The GBP are typically updated once a year to reflect the development and growth of the global Green Bond market and the discussion below is based on the version of the GBP that went into effect as of June 2018.[42]

The GBP begin by defining Green Bonds as "any type of bond instrument where the proceeds will be exclusively applied to finance or refinance, in part or in full, new and/or existing eligible Green Projects and which are aligned with the four core components of the GBP." The GBP recognized four types of Green Bonds, noting that additional types may emerge as the market develops[43]:

- *Standard Green Use of Proceeds Bond*: a standard recourse-to-the-issuer debt obligation aligned with the GBP
- *Green Revenue Bond*: a non-recourse-to-the-issuer debt obligation aligned with the GBP in which the credit exposure in the bond is to the pledged cash flows of the revenue

---

[41] The Meaning of Green, *The Economist*, September 19, 2020, 70.

[42] *Green Bond Principles: Voluntary Process Guidelines for Issuing Green Bonds*. (Paris: International Capital Market Association, June 2018).

[43] For further information on specific issuances and instruments, see the ICMA's extensive database of Green, Social and Sustainability Bonds at https://icmagroup.org/green-social-and-sustainability-bonds/green-social-and-sustainability-bonds-database/#HomeContent

streams, fees, taxes etc., and whose use of proceeds goes to related or unrelated Green Project(s)

- *Green Project Bond*: a project bond for a single or multiple Green Project(s) for which the investor has direct exposure to the risk of the project(s) with or without potential recourse to the issuer, and that is aligned with the GBP
- *Green Securitized Bond*: a bond collateralized by one or more specific Green Project(s), including but not limited to covered bonds, ABS, MBS, and other structures; and aligned with the GBP. The first source of repayment is generally the cash flows of the assets.

The GBP explicitly recognize several broad categories of eligibility for Green Projects based on their contribution to environmental objectives including climate change mitigation, climate change adaptation, natural resource conservation, biodiversity conservation, and pollution prevention and control. These categories include, but are not limited to, the following[44]:

- Renewable energy (including production, transmission, appliances and products)
- Energy efficiency (such as in new and refurbished buildings, energy storage, district heating, smart grids, appliances, and products)

---

[44] Explanation on how each of the Green Project categories can be mapped to the five overriding environmental objectives is provided in Green Project Mapping (Paris: International Capital Market Association, June 2019). In addition, reference should be made to Green and Social Bonds: A High-level Mapping to the Sustainable Development Goals (Paris: International Capital Market Association) as a frame of reference for demonstrating how the GBPs compliment the UN Sustainable Development Goals (SDGs) and evaluating the financing objectives of a Green Bond or Green Bond Program against the SDGs. For example, the GBP project category "climate change adaptation" compliments SDG 1 (No Poverty) with relevant indicators including the number of people provided access to clean energy as a result of the use of proceeds from the Green Bond.

- Pollution prevention and control (including reduction of air emissions, greenhouse gas control, soil remediation, waste prevention, waste reduction, waste recycling, and energy/emission-efficient waste to energy)
- Environmentally sustainable management of living
- Natural resources and land use (including environmentally sustainable agriculture; environmentally sustainable animal husbandry; climate smart farm inputs such as biological crop protection or drip-irrigation; environmentally sustainable fishery and aquaculture; environmentally sustainable forestry, including afforestation or reforestation, and preservation or restoration of natural landscapes)
- Terrestrial and aquatic biodiversity conservation (including the protection of coastal, marine, and watershed environments)
- Clean transportation (such as electric, hybrid, public, rail, nonmotorized, multimodal transportation, infrastructure for clean energy vehicles, and reduction of harmful emissions)
- Sustainable water and wastewater management (including sustainable infrastructure for clean and/or drinking water, wastewater treatment, sustainable urban drainage systems and river training, and other forms of flooding mitigation)
- Climate change adaptation (including information support systems, such as climate observation and early warning systems)
- Eco-efficient and/or circular economy adapted products, production technologies, and processes (such as development and introduction of environmentally sustainable products, with an eco-label or environmental certification, resource-efficient packaging, and distribution)
- Green buildings that meet regional, national, or internationally recognized standards or certifications

The four components of the GBP are as follows:

- *Use of Proceeds:* The GBP explain that the cornerstone of a Green Bond is utilization of the proceeds of the bond for

Green Projects, which should be appropriately described in the legal documentation for the security. The GBP require that all designated Green Projects provide clear environmental benefits, which will be assessed and, where feasible, quantified by the issuer.

- *Process for Project Evaluation and Selection:* The issuer of a Green Bond should clearly communicate to investors: the environmental sustainability objectives; the process by which the issuer determines how the projects fit within the eligible Green Project categories identified above; and the related eligibility criteria, including, if applicable, exclusion criteria or any other process applied to identify and manage potentially material environmental and social risks associated with the projects.
- *Management of Proceeds:* The net proceeds of the Green Bond, or an amount equal to these net proceeds, should be credited to a subaccount, moved to a sub-portfolio or otherwise tracked by the issuer in an appropriate manner, and attested to by the issuer in a formal internal process linked to the issuer's lending and investment operations for Green Projects.
- *Reporting:* Issuers should make, and keep, readily available up-to-date information on the use of proceeds to be renewed annually until full allocation, and on a timely basis in case of material developments. The annual report should include a list of the projects to which Green Bond proceeds have been allocated, as well as a brief description of the projects and the amounts allocated, and their expected impact.

The GBP include a recommendation to issuers of Green Bonds that they select and appoint external review providers to confirm the alignment of their Green Bond or bond program with the four components of the GBP. The GBP noted that issuers could seek advice from consultants and/ or institutions with recognized expertise in environmental sustainability or other aspects of the issuance of a Green Bond and also commission one of more of the various types of independent external reviews that are offered in the marketplace including second party opinions, verification, certification, and/or Green Bond scoring/rating. The GBP recommend public disclosure of external reviews that include disclosures of the credentials and relevant expertise of the external review provider and the scope of the review conducted.

Social Bonds

The proceeds of Social Bonds are used for new and existing projects with positive social outcomes (e.g., to finance or refinance loans granted to clients whose activities contribute to local economic development across the employment conservation and creation category).[45] Social Bonds provide capital for addressing issues in underserved or underprivileged sectors such as affordable housing, education, vocational training, and microfinancing, and are recognized as suitable for use in enabling, developing, and implementing new and existing projects with a positive social outcome for target populations with disadvantages including disabilities, marginalized communities, and lack of access to education. The first Social Bond, "Banking on Women," was launched in 2013 by the International Finance Corporation, which also issued a Social Bond on "Inclusive Business." While the market for Social Bonds has grown steadily, generally as a result of issuances by multinational organizations, it initially suffered from the lack of transparency and accountability and difficulties in defining and measuring social impact. While steps have been taken to address these issues, notably the development of Social Bond Principles by the ICMA, larger investors still prefer financial gains and corporations have been relatively slow to use Social Bonds as financing instruments.[46]

The ICMA's Social Bond Principles: Voluntary Process Guidelines for Issuing Social Bonds (SBP) are intended to promote integrity in the

---

[45] https://icmagroup.org/green-social-and-sustainability-bonds/ and ESG Bond Market Key topics and trends for 2019 and beyond – getting the harmony right, BBVA (July 23, 2019), https://bbva.com/wp-content/uploads/2019/07/Green-Bonds-Getting-the-harmony-right.pdf

[46] For additional information about Social Bonds and social impact investment generally, see The Social Bond market: towards a new asset class? 2018 (Impact Investment Lab, 2018), http://oecd.org/sti/ind/social-impact-investment.htm and https://ifc.org/wps/wcm/connect/corp_ext_content/ifc_external_corporate_site/about+ifc_new/investor+relations/ir-products/socialbonds

Social Bond Market through guidelines that recommend transparency, disclosure, and reporting. The SBP are updated when necessary to reflect the development and growth of the global Social Bond market and the discussion below is based on the version of the SBP that went into effect as of June 2020.[47] The SBP begin by defining Social Bonds as "any type of bond instrument where the proceeds will be exclusively applied to finance or re-finance in part or in full new and/or existing eligible Social Projects and which are aligned with the four core components of the SBP." The SBP recognized four types of Social Bonds, noting that additional types may emerge as the market develops[48]:

- *Standard Social Use of Proceeds Bond*: a standard recourse-to-the-issuer debt obligation aligned with the SBP
- *Social Revenue Bond*: a non-recourse-to-the-issuer debt obligation aligned with the SBP in which the credit exposure in the bond is to the pledged cash flows of the revenue streams, fees, taxes and so on., and whose use of proceeds go to related or unrelated Social Project(s)
- *Social Project Bond*: a project bond for a single or multiple Social Project(s) for which the investor has direct exposure to the risk of the project(s) with or without potential recourse to the issuer, and that is aligned with the SBP
- *Social Securitized and Covered Bond*: a bond collateralized by one or more specific Social Project(s), including but not limited to covered bonds, ABS, MBS, and other structures; and aligned with the SBP. The first source of repayment is generally the cash flows of the assets. This type of bond covers, for example, covered bonds backed by social housing, hospitals, or schools.

---

[47] *Social Bond Principles: Voluntary Process Guidelines for Issuing Social Bonds.* (Paris: International Capital Market Association, June 2020).

[48] For further information on specific issuances and instruments, see the ICMA's extensive database of Green, Social and Sustainability Bonds at https://icmagroup. org/green-social-and-sustainability-bonds/green-social-and-sustainability-bonds-database/#HomeContent

The SBP explains that Social Projects directly aim to address or mitigate a specific social issue and/or seek to achieve positive social outcomes especially but not exclusively for a target population(s) and describes a "social issue" as an issue that threatens, hinders, or damages the well-being of society or a specific target population. The SBP includes the following list of Social Project categories that seeks to capture the most commonly used types of projects supported by or expected to be supported by the Social Bond market[49]:

- Affordable basic infrastructure (e.g. clean drinking water, sewers, sanitation, transport, energy)
- Access to essential services (e.g. health, education and vocational training, healthcare, financing and financial services)
- Affordable housing
- Employment generation, and programs designed to prevent and/or alleviate unemployment stemming from socioeconomic crises, including through the potential effect of small- and medium-sized enterprise financing and microfinance
- Food security and sustainable food systems (e.g. physical, social, and economic access to safe, nutritious, and sufficient food that meets dietary needs and requirements; resilient agricultural practices; reduction of food loss and waste; and improved productivity of small-scale producers)

---

[49] The SBP noted that Social Projects include attempts to provide and/or promote the goals in one or more of the categories and all related and supporting expenditures such as research and development. Reference should be made to *Green and Social Bonds: A High-level Mapping to the Sustainable Development Goals* (Paris: International Capital Market Association) as a frame of reference for demonstrating how the SBPs compliment the UN Sustainable Development Goals (SDGs) and evaluating the financing objectives of a Social Bond or Social Bond Program against the SDGs. For example, the SBP project categories "access to essential services," "affordable housing," and "socioeconomic advancement and empowerment" compliment SDG 1 (No Poverty) with relevant indicators including number of products and services serving low-income groups and the number of people provided with access to financial services, including microfinance, as a result of the use of proceeds from the Social Bond.

- Socioeconomic advancement and empowerment (e.g. equitable access to and control over assets, services, resources, and opportunities; equitable participation and integration into the market and society, including reduction of income inequality)

The SEP noted that examples of target populations include, but are not limited to, those that are:

- Living below the poverty line
- Excluded and/or marginalized populations and/or communities
- People with disabilities
- Migrants and/or displaced persons
- Undereducated
- Underserved, owing to a lack of quality access to essential goods and services
- Unemployed
- Women and/or sexual and gender minorities
- Aging populations and vulnerable youth
- Other vulnerable groups, including as a result of natural disasters

The four components of the SBP are as follows:

- *Use of Proceeds:* The SBP explain that the cornerstone of a Social Bond is utilization of the proceeds of the bond for Social Projects, which should be appropriately described in the legal documentation for the security. The SBP require that all designated Social Projects provide clear social benefits, which will be assessed and, where feasible, quantified by the issuer.
- *Process for Project Evaluation and Selection:* The issuer of a Social Bond should clearly communicate to investors: the social objectives; the process by which the issuer determines how the projects fit within the eligible Social Project categories identified above; and the related eligibility

criteria, including, if applicable, exclusion criteria or any
other process applied to identify and manage potentially
material environmental and social risks associated with
the projects.

- *Management of Proceeds:* The net proceeds of the Social
Bond, or an amount equal to these net proceeds, should
be credited to a sub-account, moved to a sub-portfolio, or
otherwise tracked by the issuer in an appropriate manner,
and attested to by the issuer in a formal internal process
linked to the issuer's lending and investment operations for
Social Projects.

- *Reporting:* Issuers should make and keep readily available
up-to-date information on the use of proceeds to be renewed
annually until full allocation, and on a timely basis in case of
material developments. The annual report should include a
list of the projects to which Social Bond proceeds have been
allocated, as well as a brief description of the projects and the
amounts allocated, and their expected impact.

As is the case with Green Bonds, the SBP include a recommendation
to issuers of Social Bonds that they seek advice from consultants and/
or institutions with recognized expertise in social issues or other aspects
of the issuance of a Social Bond and select and appoint external review
providers to confirm the alignment of their Social Bond or bond program
with the four components of the SBP. The SBP also recommends public
disclosure of external reviews that include disclosures of the credentials
and relevant expertise of the external review provider and the scope of the
review conducted.

Sustainability Bonds

Sustainability Bonds encompass elements from both Green and Social
Bonds and are used implement a combination of positive environmental
and social impact and for both environmental and social projects in a variety of categories including food health and well-being, quality education,

clean water and sanitation, affordable, and clean energy.[50] When issuing its Sustainability Bond Guidelines in June 2018, the ICMA described Sustainability Bonds as bonds where the proceeds will be exclusively applied to finance or refinance a combination of both Green and Social Projects (as those terms are defined and explained in the GBP and the SBP), noting that a market has developed for bonds aligned with both the GBP and the SBP).[51]

The ICMA explained that Sustainability Bonds are aligned with the four core components of both the GBP and the SBP (with the former being especially relevant to underlying Green Projects and the latter to underlying Social Projects) and that those common four core components of the GBP and the SBP and their recommendations on the use of external reviews and impact reporting also apply to Sustainability Bonds. One form of Sustainability Bond is a Social Impact Bond, which is based on a "pay-for-success model" enabled by public–private partnerships. In a typical situation, a private sector investor provides funds to a local party that will be responsible for implementing a specific social project so as to achieve mutually agreed impact performance targets. At the end of the project, its impacts are measured by an outside outcome evaluator and if the targets are achieved the investors will be paid by the local government as provided under the terms of the bond.

Sustainability-Linked Bonds

In its Sustainability-Linked Bond Principles (SLBP) released in June 2020, the ICMA described Sustainability-Linked Bonds (SLBs) as any type of bond instrument for which the financial and/or structural characteristics can vary depending on whether the issuer achieves predefined

[50] https://icmagroup.org/green-social-and-sustainability-bonds/ and ESG Bond Market Key topics and trends for 2019 and beyond – getting the harmony right, BBVA (July 23, 2019), https://bbva.com/wp-content/uploads/2019/07/Green-Bonds-Getting-the-harmony-right.pdf

[51] *Sustainability Bond Guidelines* (Paris: International Capital Market Association, June 2018).

Sustainability/ESG objectives, which are measured through predefined Key Performance Indicators (KPIs) and assessed against predefined Sustainability Performance Targets (SPTs).[52] The proceeds of SLBs are intended to be used for general purposes, thus the use of proceeds is not a determinant of its categorization; however, issuers can elect to combine the GBP/SBP approaches with their SLB.[53] There are five core components to the SLBP:

- *Selection of KPIs:* KPIs that can be external or internal; however, they must always be material to the issuer's core sustainability and business strategy and address relevant ESG challenges of the industry that are under management's control. Specifically, KPIs should be relevant, core, and material to the issuer's overall business, and of high strategic significance to the issuer's current and/or future operations; measurable or quantifiable on a consistent methodological basis; externally verifiable and able to be benchmarked using an external reference or definitions to facilitate the assessment of the SPT's level of ambition.[54]
- *Calibration of SPTs:* Issuers must calibrate and set in good faith one or more SPT(s) per KPI that represent their commitment to ambitious change and which represent a material improvement in the respective KPIs and be beyond a "business as usual" trajectory; where possible be compared to a benchmark or an external reference; be consistent with the

---

[52] The discussion of the SLBP and SLBs in this section is adapted from *Sustainability-Linked Bond Principles: Voluntary Process Guidelines* (Paris: International Capital Market Association, June 2020).

[53] The SLBP noted that SLBs should not be confused with Sustainability Bonds, which require that the Use of Proceeds conform to the Sustainability Bond Guidelines.

[54] The SLBP encourages issuers, when possible, to select KPI(s) that they have already included in their previous annual reports, sustainability reports, or other nonfinancial reporting disclosures to allow investors to evaluate historical performance of the KPIs selected. When KPIs that have not been previously disclosed are used, issuers should, to the extent possible, provide historical externally verified KPI values covering at least the previous three years.

issuers' overall strategic sustainability/ESG strategy and be determined on a predefined timeline, set before (or concurrently with) the issuance of the bond. The SLBP provides that target setting should be based on a combination of benchmarking approaches: the issuer's own performance over time on the selected KPIs (a minimum of three years, where feasible, is recommended); relative positioning versus the performance of the issuers' peers or versus current industry or sector standards; and/or reference to the science, official country/regional/international targets (e.g., Paris Agreement on Climate Change and net zero goals, Sustainable Development Goals (SDGs), etc.) or recognized best-available technologies.

- *Bond Characteristics:* The SLB must describe when and how the bond's financial and/or structural characteristics will vary based on whether or not the selected KPI(s) reach the predefined SPT(s). The SLBP noted that potential variation of the coupon was the most common example of variation, but that it was also possible to consider the variation of other financial and/or structural characteristics of the SLB.

- *Reporting:* The SLBP call on issuers of SLBs to regularly publish (at least annually) and keep readily available and easily accessible, up-to-date information on the performance of the selected KPI(s), including baselines where relevant; a verification assurance report relative to the SPT outlining the performance against the SPTs and the related impact, and timing of such impact, on the bond's financial and/or structural characteristics; and any information enabling investors to monitor the level of ambition of the SPTs (e.g., any update in the issuers sustainability strategy or on the related KPI/ESG governance, and more generally any information relevant to the analysis of the KPIs and SPTs).

- *Verification:* The SLBP requires issuers of SLBs to seek independent and external verification (e.g., limited or reasonable assurance) of their performance level against each SPT for each KPI by a qualified external reviewer with relevant expertise (e.g., auditor or an environmental consultant), at least once a year, and in any case for any date/period relevant for

assessing the SPT performance leading to a potential adjust-
ment of the SLB financial and/or structural characteristics,
until after the last SPT trigger event of the bond has been
reached. Performance verifications should be made publicly
available.

Disclosures regarding the processes used and assumptions underlying
the KPIs and SPTs are obviously important. The SLBP calls on issuers
to communicate clearly to investors the rationale and process according
to which the KPI(s) have been selected and how the KPI(s) fit into their
sustainability strategy, and to provide clear definitions of the KPI(s) that
include the applicable scope or perimeter (e.g., the percentage of the issuer's total emissions to which the target is applicable) and the calculation
methodology (e.g., clear definition of the denominator of intensity-based
KPIs and definition of a baseline, where feasible, that is science-based or
benchmarked against an industry standard). With respect to calibrating
and setting their SPTs, issuers are expected to disclose to investors any
strategic information that may decisively impact the achievement of the
SPTs and clearly refer to each of the following:

- The timelines for the target achievement, including the target
  observation date(s)/period(s), the trigger event(s), and the
  frequency of SPTs
- Where relevant, the verified baseline or reference point
  selected for improvement of KPIs as well as the rationale
  for that baseline or reference point to be used (including
  date/period)
- Where relevant, in what situations recalculations or pro-forma
  adjustments of baselines will take place
- Where possible and taking competition and confidentiality
  considerations into account, how the issuer intends to reach
  such SPTs (e.g., by describing its ESG strategy, supporting
  ESG governance and investments, and its operating strategy
  (i.e., the types of actions that are expected to drive the issuer's
  performance toward achievement of the SPTs))
- Any other key factors beyond the issuer's direct control that
  may affect the achievement of the SPT(s)

The SLBP also encourages issuers to position the information outlined above within the context of their overarching objectives, strategy, policy, and/or processes relating to ESG.[55] Appendix II of the SLBP is a guiding, nonexhaustive checklist of elements that are recommended or required to be disclosed in the context of the issuance of an SLB with respect to selection of KPIs, calibration of SPTs, bond characteristics, reporting commitments, second party opinions, and post-issuance reporting and verification. The SLBP noted that disclosures may be included in the bond documentation and, where appropriate, in a standalone document such as a framework, investor presentation, external review, or on issuers' website or annual sustainability or annual reports.

International and Regional Sustainable Finance Initiatives

In February 2020, the International Capital Markets Association (ICMA) published *Sustainable Finance: Compendium of International Policy Initiatives and Best Market Practice* (https://icmagroup.org/green-social-and-sustainability-bonds/sustainable-finance-initiatives/) with the goal of providing stakeholders with an easy reference point to the numerous international and regional developments in the field. Among the international initiatives highlighted were the following:

- The Corporate Forum on Sustainable Finance: The Forum was established in January 2019 by sixteen European Union (EU) companies with the intent of becoming a permanent network of dynamic "Green Issuers" for exchanging views and ideas relating to upholding and developing sustainable finance as a critical tool to fight climate change and to foster a more sustainable and responsible society.

---

[55] The SLBP recommend that, in connection with the issuance of an SLB, issuers appoint (an) external review provider(s) to confirm the alignment of their bond with the five core components of the SLBP (e.g., a Second Party Opinion) and that external reviewers assess the relevance, robustness and reliability of selected KPIs, the rationale and level of ambition of the proposed SPTs, the relevance and reliability of selected benchmarks and baselines and the credibility of the strategy outlined to achieve them, based on scenario analyses, where relevant.

- The Global Green Finance Council: The Council was created in 2017 with the objective to bring together key global and regional associations and other stakeholders involved in the green financing to coordinate efforts to promote green finance, facilitate cross-fertilization between related markets and asset classes, and act as a representative counterparty to the official sector on green finance policy matters.
- The Green Loan Principles (GLP): The GLP were launched in March 2018 by the Loan Market Association (LMA), together with the Asia Pacific Loan Market Association (APLMA) and with the support of the ICMA, to create a high-level framework of market standards and guidelines, providing a consistent methodology for use across the wholesale green loan market.
- The Sustainability Linked Loan Principles (SLLP): The SLLP were launched in March 2019 by the LMA, together with the APLMA and the Loan Syndications and Trading Association (LSTA) and with the support of the ICMA, to promote and facilitate the use of the sustainability linked loan product.
- The Green Bond Pledge: The Green Bond Pledge is a simple declaration with broad and far-reaching impact that was developed and designed as a joint initiative by a wide range of international climate finance and environmental groups including the Climate Bonds Initiative, Mission 2020, Ceres, Citizens Climate Lobby, California Governor's Office, California Treasurer's Office, Global Optimism, NRDC, and The Climate Group.
- Network of Central Banks and Supervisors for Greening the Financial System (NGFS): The NGFS was established at the Paris "One Planet Summit" in December 2017 by eight central banks and supervisors to help strengthening the global response required to meet the goals of the Paris agreement and to enhance the role of the financial system to manage risks and to mobilize capital for green and low-carbon investments in the broader context of environmentally sustainable development.

- The Sustainable Stock Exchanges (SSE): The SSE initiative was launched in 2009 by the UN Secretary General and organized by UNCTAD, the UN Global Compact, UNEP FI, and the PRI to provide a global platform for exploring how exchanges, in collaboration with investors, companies (issuers), regulators, policymakers, and relevant international organizations can enhance performance on ESG issues and encourage sustainable investment, including the financing of the UN Sustainable Development Goals.

Other international initiatives mentioned included the Financial Stability Board—Task Force on Climate-related Financial Disclosures, the G20 Sustainable Finance Study Group, the Sustainable Banking Network and the Equator Principles.

As for regional developments, notice should be taken of a wide range of initiatives in the ASEAN Market including the issuance of Green Bond Standards, ASEAN Social Bond Standards, and ASEAN Sustainability Standards by the ASEAN Capital Markets Forum, which also produced a December 2018 document on *Aligning Sustainable Finance with the Sustainable Development Goals*. The Green Bond Guidelines (2017) were introduced in Japan in March 2017 to facilitate sustainable finance and Green Bond issuances in that country. The European Commission has announced work on developing an EU classification system to determine whether an economic activity is environmentally sustainable, an EU Green Bond Standard and guidance to improve disclosures of climate-related information by businesses. In addition, other countries that have issued guidelines relating to Green Bonds include Brazil, China, Kenya, Malaysia and the Philippines.

Swiss Sustainable Finance (www.sustainablefinance.ch) compiled a list of sustainable investing standards that included Eurosif Transparency Code, Febelfin Quality Standard and Label (Belgium), FNG-Label for Sustainable Mutual Funds, FNG Sustainability Profiles and Transparency Matrix Luxflag ESG label, Nordic Swan Ecolabel for Investment Funds, Greenfin Label (France) and Label ISR (France).

CHAPTER 2

What Is Impact Investing?

Impact investing is aimed directly at creating a positive environmental or social impact by identifying and solving a particular environmental or social problem. Impact investing is an advanced stage of sustainable investing that began with the socially responsible investment movement that emerged in the 1970s and which was marked by the use of negative or exclusionary screening processes designed to avoid specific assets due to consideration of specific environmental, social, and governance (ESG) criteria including moral values (e.g., tobacco or gambling), standards and norms (e.g., human rights), ethical convictions (e.g., animal testing), or legal requirements (e.g., controversial armaments such as cluster bombs or land mines, excluded in order to comply with international conventions). The next stage was based on "best-in-class" (positive) screening, which contrasts significantly with negative screening and calls for investment and lending decisions to be made based on demonstrated high ESG performance of sectors, companies, or projects and adherence to minimum standards of business practice based on international norms relating to climate protection, human rights, working conditions, and action plans against corruption.

As time went by, investors began to use positive screening in a more focused manner by concentrating their activities on specific high-profile sustainability-related themes such as clean tech, infrastructure, affordable housing, energy-efficient real estate or sustainable forestry.[1] BNP Paribas (BNP) referred to the rise of social impact investing, sometimes referred to as social finance or solidary-based finance, which includes investments

---

[1] Krauss, A., P. Kruger and J. Meyer. September 2016. *Sustainable Finance in Switzerland: Where Do We Stand?* 18–19. Zurich: Sustainable Finance Institute; Environmental, Social and Governance Issues in Investing: 2015. A Guide for Investment Professionals. CFA Institute; and Changing Dynamics of Sustainable Finance: The Regulatory Push in the Direction of Sustainable Growth, Sia Partners. February 25, 2020. https://sia-partners.com/en/news-and-publications/from-our-experts/changing-dynamics-sustainable-finance-regulatory-push

into projects that have a social focus and seek to address a particular social or environmental challenge such as housing problems caused by increased poverty, unemployment, environmental issues such as organic farming or clean energy and development of third world economies.[2] Other drivers of maturation of the sustainable investment marketplace have included the development of new and emerging methodologies intended to systematically and explicitly include ESG risks and opportunities into traditional financial-based investment analysis and the growing role of "active ownership," which focuses on engagement and dialogue with portfolio companies after an initial investment is made in order to influence ESG strategies and actions through exercise of ownership rights and being a visible activist for change.[3]

The term "impact investing" was coined by the Rockefeller Foundation in 2007 and today the most commonly used definition is the one proposed by the Global Impact Investment Network (GIIN) (https://thegiin.org/impact-investing/): "investing made with the intention to generate positive, measurable social and environmental impact alongside a financial return." A similar formulation was adopted by the G8's Social Impact Investment Taskforce: "the defining characteristic of impact investment is that the goal of generating financial returns is unequivocally pursued within the context of setting impact objectives and measuring their achievement," and the Taskforce also declared: "The world is on the brink of a revolution in how we solve society's toughest problems. The force capable of driving this revolution is 'social impact investing,' which harnesses entrepreneurship, innovation and capital to power social improvement."[4] BNP has noted that impact investing, like microfinance

---

[2] https://group.bnpparibas/en/news/sustainable-finance-about. For further information on social impact investing, see the website of Finansol (https://finansol.org/en/index.php), a French organization that certifies certain social finance products and monitors trends in social finance.

[3] Krauss, A., P. Kruger, and J. Meyer. September 2016. *Sustainable Finance in Switzerland: Where Do We Stand?* 18–19. Zurich: Sustainable Finance Institute.

[4] Impact Investment: The Invisible Heart of Markets. 2014. Social Impact Investment Taskforce, 18. The Taskforce was convened in 2013 to bring together governmental and sectoral experts from the G7 countries, the European Commission and Australia to discuss and report on recommendations for "catalyzing a global market in impact investment."

and social impact bonds (i.e., bonds that are repaid upon maturation only if the social objectives of the project have been achieved), is focused on "social businesses," which were described by BNP as being primarily social in nature but following viable economic models—in other words, a shared value concept that seeks both profit and social impact.[5] As for what "impact" might be in this context, the term has been defined as "any meaningful change in the economic, social, cultural, environmental and/or political condition due to specific actions and behavioral changes by individuals, communities and/or society as a whole."[6]

Impact investing has also been explained to include a range of investment opportunities that exist between traditional investing, which focuses on maximizing profits, and philanthropy, which has generally been undertaken to achieve environmental or social good with regard for financial returns. Singh explained that unlike traditional investing, which focuses only on financial data, sustainable investing (including impact investing) also considers and manages ESG metrics in order to generate long-term value and reduce risk.[7] Impact investing has been aligned with the concept of venture philanthropy, which has been described as the application or redirection of principles of traditional venture capital financing to achieve philanthropic endeavors.[8] According to Singh, venture philanthropy and impact investing comprise a broader category called "concessionary investing" that includes projects that produce social

[5] https://group.bnpparibas/en/news/sustainable-finance-about. BNP noted that with the consent of investors profits generated from impact investment projects may be reinvested to combat exclusion, protect the environment or promote development and solidarity.

[6] Godeke, S., and P. Briaud. 2020. *Impact Investing Handbook: An Implementation Guide for Practitioners*, 8. Rockefeller Philanthropy Advisors, See also Burand, D. 2015. "Resolving Impact Investment Disputes: When Doing Good Goes Bad." *Washington University Journal of Law & Policy* 48, pp. 55–57 (Note 6) ("Some observers trace impact investing's roots in the United States to 1950, when the United States started selling political risk insurance to US companies investing abroad.")

[7] See Singh, J. 2020. "Maximizing Outcomes in Impact Investing." March 26, 2020, https://knowledge.insead.edu/strategy/maximising-outcomes-in-impact-investing-13636

[8] https://investopedia.com/terms/v/venture-philanthropy.asp

impact but only generating below-market expected financial returns. He notes that while this result may be satisfactory for certain types of impact investors, such as relatively inexperienced high-net-worth individuals, foundations or development agencies, banks and pension funds that need to deliver strong financial returns must engage in "non-concessionary investing," an approach that has been criticized as steering asset managers too far away from ensuring real environmental and social impact and diverting capital away from social enterprises working on innovative market-based solutions in difficult contexts.

Impact investing has occurred in both emerging and developed markets and, as discussed above, the goals of impact investors in committing their capital and ancillary resources have ranged from market-driven risk-adjusted returns to concessional and capital preservation. Impact investing has occurred in a broad range of sectors including sustainable agriculture, renewable energy, conservation, and microfinance, and governments and private enterprises have turned to impact investing tools to address challenges that have arisen relating to the delivery of basic services such as housing, health care, and education to underserved individuals or communities.

The GIIN has identified the following core characteristics of impact investing[9]:

- *Intentionality:* Impact investors invest with the intent to have a positive social or environmental impact through their investments.
- *Expectation of Financial Returns:* Impact investments are not grants that do not need to be repaid: investors expect a financial return on their capital or, at minimum, a return of their capital.
- *Range of Return Expectations and Asset Classes:* Impact investments target financial returns that range from below-market to risk-adjusted market rate (two-thirds of the capital for impact investment seeks risk-adjusted market rates) and can

---

[9] See Core Characteristics of Impact Investing. 2019. Global Impact Investment Network. https://thegiin.org/assets/Core%20Characteristics_webfile.pdf

be made across asset classes, including but not limited to cash equivalents, fixed income, venture capital, and private equity.

- *Impact Measurement:* A hallmark of impact investing is the commitment of the investor to measure and report the social and environmental performance and progress of underlying investments, ensuring transparency and accountability while informing the practice of impact investing and building the field.

Similarly, Godeke and Briaud argued that the two key elements from the GIIN definition of impact investment are intention and measurement. As for intention, they explained that investors must have the intention to achieve both financial returns and positive social or environmental impact when making decisions about how their invested assets are to be used. An investment in a project such as electronic car manufacturing that is made solely with the intention to promote a positive social impact is important, but does not meet the standard of intention since the investor is not acting with the intent to achieve a financial return. As for measurement, investors must explicitly measure both the financial performance of their investments and the environmental and/or social impact of the investments, which is admittedly a challenge given that measurement tools for environmental and/or social impact have yet to develop to the level that investors have come to expect for gauging financial returns. Godeke and Briaud pointed out that enterprises launched to pursue an environmental or social purpose and goals can, and often do, benefit from the support of both impact investors (as defined above) and other investors that do not fall within the definition because they are only interested in a financial return or impact.[10] They also noted that some impact investors use another variable that has been referred to as "contribution," or "additionality," and which is a kind of "but for" question

---

[10] Godeke, S., and P. Briaud. 2020. *Impact Investing Handbook: An Implementation Guide for Practitioners*, 28–30. Rockefeller Philanthropy Advisors. (includes a table that describes how the International Finance Corporation assessed the degree to which specific asset classes have the impact investing attributes of intent, contribution (explained below) and measurement).

that asks whether a particular investment will cause "an increase in the quantity or quality of the enterprise's social outcomes beyond what would have otherwise occurred."[11]

The GIIN has noted that since impact investing is a relatively new term, used to describe investments made across many asset classes, sectors and regions, it has been challenging to develop a rigorous methodology for estimating the total size of the market. The GIIN has been working to strengthen its database and methodology and released its 2020 Annual Impact Investor Survey that included an estimate that over 1,720 organizations were managing $715 billion in impact investing assets under management (AUM) as of the end of 2019.[12] Established companies have been compelled to respond to calls by institutional investors to incorporate responsible ESG initiatives into their business models as a condition to continued support in public capital markets. Other companies seeking to demonstrate to impact investors their commitment to environmental and social responsibility have opted for emerging forms of legal entities, so-called social enterprises, which explicitly incorporate sustainability and multistakeholder interests into their governance and reporting frameworks.

Impact investing has been characterized as an attempt to incorporate an evidence-based mechanism for measuring accountability into giving, a move driven by the evolution of philanthropy from charitable giving from foundations and philanthropists to development financial corporations, multilateral banks, and impact-focused asset managers.[13] Impact investment is the smallest by assets among the various categories of sustainable financing, but it has attracted a lot of attention in recent years

---

[11] Id. (quotation taken from Brest, P., and K. Born. 2013. "Unpacking the Impact in Impact Investing." *Stanford Social Innovation Review: Informing and Inspiring Leaders of Social Change*). Godeke and Briaud conceded that the inclusion of "contribution" as one the hard boundaries of what constitutes an impact investment is still being debated.

[12] https://thegiin.org/impact-investing/need-to-know/#how-big-is-the-impact-investing-market. According to GIIN's 2019 Annual Impact Investment Survey the size of impact AUM grew by a 17% compound annual growth rate from 2015 to 2019.

[13] Sustainable Finance (The middle Road), https://themiddleroad.org/sustainable-finance-unleashed/

and is perceived to be the most ambitious of all of the strategies. A project is only suitable for impact investment if it is feasible to quantify and measure its precise environmental and/or social impact (e.g., the reduction in the volume of carbon dioxide emitted during the course of the company's operations or the number of girls within a certain age group that gain access to education in a particular village).[14]

In the early days of impact investing only small, niche firms participated; however, the last few years has seen a dramatic rise in interest among larger players such as BlackRock, Goldman Sachs, Bain Capital, and TPG, all of which have launched funds or offered other opportunities to investors focused on ESG.[15] A wide range of individual and institutional investors that have entered the impact investment marketplace including fund managers, development finance institutions, diversified financial institutions/banks, private foundations, pension funds and insurance companies, private funds, hybrid funds, ethical banks, microfinance institutions, social stock exchanges, crowdfunding, government institutions, family offices, individual investors, nongovernmental organizations (NGOs) and religious institutions. Continued growing enthusiasm can be expected given that feedback from investors indicated that portfolio performance has generally met or exceed their expectations for both social and environmental impact and financial return; however, access to capital from impact investors may be limited for companies that lack scalable high-quality investment projects.

Global Impact Trends and Initiatives

While, as mentioned above, the term "impact investing" was first used and popularized in 2007 by the Rockefeller Foundation, the concept of integrating nonfinancial values and goals into investing has a long history. Some of the events highlighted in a short "modern history of impact investing" include the launch of the first socially responsible investment mutual fund by Pax World in 1971; the launch of the Forum

---

[14] The Economist explains: What is Sustainable Finance? The Economist. April 17, 2018, https://economist.com/the-economist-explains/2018/04/17/what-is-sustainable-finance

[15] Id.

for Sustainable and Responsible Investment in 1984; the issuance of
the Brundtland Report *Our Common Future* in 1987, which provided the
foundation for what has become the "sustainable development" movement; the creation of what is now called the MSCI KLD 400 Social Index
in 1990; the introduction of the UN Principles for Responsible Investment (unpri.org) in 2006; and the launch of GIIN in 2009.[16] Over the
last decade impact investing has continued to emerge and evolve amid
a range of global economic, social, and political trends and initiatives
intended to create a legal and regulatory framework within which impact
investing can be conducted. Examples include the following:

- Maryland was the first state in the United States to pass
  "benefit corporation" legislation in 2010 and since then a
  majority of the states and the District of Columbia have
  adopted statutes that permit the formation of this new form
  of for-profit corporation that explicitly expands the fiduciary
  duties of directors beyond maximizing shareholder value,
  which has been the traditional standard of corporate governance, to include consideration of whether or not the corporation's activities have an overall positive impact on society,
  their workers, the communities in which they operate, and
  the environment.[17] Benefit corporations have been formed to
  explicitly pursue and produce a particular public benefit, such
  as promoting education in the community, and have opted to

---

[16] Godeke, S., and P. Briaud. 2015. *Impact Investing Handbook: An Implementation Guide for Practitioners*, 8. Rockefeller Philanthropy Advisors. See also
Burand, D. 2015. "Resolving Impact Investment Disputes: When Doing Good
Goes Bad." *Washington University Journal of Law & Policy* 48, pp. 55–57 (Note
6) ("Some observers trace impact investing's roots in the United States to 1950,
when the United States started selling political risk insurance to US companies
investing abroad.")

[17] By 2020, over 40 states and the District of Columbia had either adopted legislation authorizing the creation of a benefit corporation or were seriously considering such legislation https://benefitcorp.net/policymakers/state-by-state-status

be accountable for their actions through disclosure requirements and external verification.

- Companies interested in publicly demonstrating their commitment to creating a positive environmental and social impact and being held accountable for their actions can seek to become a "Certified B Corporation" by fulfilling the requirements established by B Lab Company (B Lab), a Pennsylvania nonprofit corporation. In order to become "certified" a company must achieve a minimum verified score on a "B Impact Assessment" that covers financial performance; suppliers; the impact of the business on all its stakeholders; best practices regarding mission, measurement, and governance; and the company's "impact business model."

- Governments, companies, investors, and stakeholder representatives now operate in world that is full of transnational, voluntary standards for what constitutes responsible corporate actions, including standards that have been developed by states; public/private partnerships; multistakeholder negotiation processes; industry sectors and companies; institutional investors; functional groups such as accountancy firms and social assurance consulting groups; NGOs and nonfinancial ratings agencies. Notable examples include the UN Global Compact, OECD Guidelines for Multinational Enterprises, and the UN Sustainable Development Goals (SDGs), each of which include goals and/or indicators relating to businesses' environmental and social impacts.

- It is now widely acknowledged that best practices relating to the implementation of effective sustainability practices must include a commitment to transparency and reporting on sustainability-related activities and impacts to the organization's stakeholders. In addition, sustainability is like any other important strategic initiative and should be carried out pursuant to a formal sustainability management system and process that includes due diligence, development, and implementation of strategic and operational goals and plans, monitoring, and assessment of impacts overseen by the members of the governing body of the organization. Investors have come to expect, if not require, that their portfolio companies commit to adherence to one or more of the widely used sustainability-related standards that specifically address reporting and management such as the Global Reporting Initiative (www.globalreporting.org); the International Integrated Reporting Framework (integratedreporting.org); the Sustainability Accounting Standards Board standards (www.sasb.org); and the standards of the International Organization for Standardization relating to environmental management (ISO 14001) and social responsibility (ISO 26000).

- Securities exchanges and regulators have a long history of intervening in the capital raising process through the imposition of rules relating to corporate governance and the last two decades has seen a surge in regulatory initiatives around the world seeking to better integrate corporate governance and sustainability. For example, the European Union (EU) has implemented a directive that requires nearly 7,000 large companies and "public interest organizations," such as banks and insurance companies, to "prepare a nonfinancial statement containing information relating to at least environmental matters, social and employee-related matters including diversity, respect for human rights, anti-corruption and bribery matters" and individual countries in the EU have their own additional requirements (e.g., France requires listed companies to disclose their impact on social and environmental issues in their annual reports and accounts).[18] In addition, several stock exchanges around the world require social and/or environmental disclosure as part of their listing requirements

---

[18] See 6 of Directive 2014/95/EU of the European Parliament and of the Council of 22 October 2014, amending Directive 2013/34/EU as regards disclosure of non-financial and diversity information by certain large undertakings and groups, Official Journal of the European Union L330/1-330/9.

including exchanges in Australia, Brazil, Canada, India, Singapore, South Africa, and the London Stock Exchange.[19]

- Asset managers and financial institutions have responded to the demands of their own investors for more account- ability with respect to the environmental and social impacts of investment decisions by committing to relevant volun- tary standards such as the UN Principles for Responsible Investment and the Equator Principles. Also, pension funds in countries such as Australia, Belgium, Canada, France, Germany, Italy, Japan, Sweden, and the UK are required to disclose the extent to which the fund incorporates social and environmental information into their investment decisions.[20]

- Aligned with the recognition of benefit corporations based on the premise that directors owe fiduciary duties to all of the stakeholders of the business has been the steady call for the redefining the "purpose" of the corporation as being not solely about profit, but also about public purposes that relate to the company's wider contribution to public interests and societal goals.[21] In 2019 a group of 181 CEOs who were members of

---

[19] Williams, C. 2016. "Corporate Social Responsibility and Corporate Govern- ance." In *Oxford Handbook of Corporate Law and Governance*, eds. J. Gordon and G. Ringe, 16. Oxford: Oxford University Press, Available at http://digitalcom- mons.osgoode.yorku.ca/scholarly_works/1784 (citing Initiative for Responsible Investment, Corporate Social Responsibility Disclosure Efforts by National Gov- ernments and Stock Exchanges (March 12, 2015), available at http://hausercenter. org/iri/wpcontent/uploads/2011/08/CR-3-12-15.pdf). The US has been notably slower than other jurisdictions to regulate with respect to disclosures relating to environmental and social responsibility; however, the SEC has engaged in rule- making relating explanation of climate risks to their future profitability, either from physical changes associated with climate change, or from regulatory initia- tives designed to mitigate climate risk; disclosure of the ratio of the CEO's total pay to the median employee pay; mine safety disclosure; and "conflict minerals" disclosure where tin; tantalum, tungsten or gold from the Democratic Republic of the Congo or neighboring countries were incorporated into listed companies' products. Id.

[20] Id.

[21] 2019. *Principles for Purposeful Business*. London: The British Academy.

the Business Roundtable signed a statement that redefined the purpose of a corporation to include not only improving shareholder value, but also investing in employees, protecting the environment and dealing ethically with other stakeholders such as suppliers. All this has met that a brighter light will be shined on identifying and measuring the environmental and social impacts of the operations of companies.

- In Europe, several legal initiatives have been launched to support expansion of sustainable finance and impact investment including a taxonomy for sustainable economic activities to facilitate the creation of standards that can be referenced to determine whether economic activity qualifies as environmentally sustainable; adoption of requirements on investment managers to disclose how they have considered sustainability issues that materially affect an investment's value and an investment's broader societal impacts; and introduction of requirements that must be satisfied in order for financial products to be labeled "green" or "sustainable." These initiatives, and others, are essential to the success of the EU's plans for an EU Green Deal announced in December 2019.

- While the United States has been slower than other parts of the world to regulate with respect to ESG-related disclosures, there has been growing pressure on the Securities and Exchange Commission to establish a better ESG reporting framework for public companies, and legislation has been introduced at the federal level to support the development of clearer ESG metrics and reporting by public companies of their analysis and assessment of the impact of ESG factors on their businesses.[22] States such as Illinois now require public or governmental agencies that manage public funds to imple-

---

[22] It has been reported that the SEC has sent examination letters to asset managers and funds that have been marketing themselves as pursuing ESG strategies. See Fleishhacker, E., and R. 2020. *Young. Impact Investing: A Legal Primer.* Arnold & Porter Kaye Scholer LLP.

ment sustainable investment policies for those funds.[23]
States have also passed laws to address specific social issues
such as requiring gender diversity in the boardrooms of
public companies.

In addition to the trends described above, the impact investing community, like society at large, must now grapple with the fallout from the COVID-19 pandemic and the events that triggered the large-scale protests in the United States and around the world relating to racial injustice. While the COVID-19 pandemic has created an economic shock that will likely take years to overcome, significantly increasing financial risks and uncertainties for investors, it seems clear that impact investors can play an important role in responding to the pandemic by supporting businesses and the reform and strengthening of major social systems in crucial areas such as health, education, community development, and housing. The CEO of the Soros Economic Development Fund declared the pandemic to be a "seminal test for the impact investment field," and the CEO of GIIN called impact investing "more important than ever" and said that the pandemic was a time for impact investors to "lean into the moment." The chief policy officer of the Global Steering Group for

---

[23] Federal regulation relating to consideration of ESG factors by managers of private retirement plans remains controversial. Early in 2020 the Department of Labor ("DOL") announced a proposed rule that would direct retirement plan fiduciaries who manage funds under the Employment Retirement Income Security Act of 1974 that they must select plans based on financial considerations, meaning that fiduciaries would be restricted from factoring in non-pecuniary goals and that ESG factors could only be considered if the presented economic risks or opportunities and were material under generally accepted investment theories. The proposals were heavily criticized by asset managers and large investors including the Investment Company Institute, BlackRock, the Vanguard Group and State Street Global Advisors, many of which called for the proposal to be withdrawn and for the DOL to engage with industry on the subject. Among other things, comment letters on the proposal took issue with the assumption that integrating ESG is by nature non-pecuniary and suggested that any legitimate concerns could be addressed by a robust disclosure regime rather than restrictions on the discretion of asset managers. L. Weiss, "Asset managers, investors criticize Labor Dept. proposal on ESG", 2020 CQCRPGRPT 0296 (August 12, 2020).

Impact Investment said, "The way we tackle the recovery phase will shape whether we're moving to a new economic order with impact at the center."[24] The GIIN launched the Response, Recovery, and Resilience Investment Coalition, the "R3 Coalition" to streamline impact investing efforts to address the large-scale social and economic consequences of the COVID-19 pandemic and accelerate impact investments to respond, recover, and build resilience in the face of the pandemic. With respect to the role of impact investors in addressing systemic racism, 128 institutional investors signed on to a statement issued by the Racial Justice Investing (https://racialjusticeinvesting.org/) coalition that recognized that the investor community had contributed to, and benefited from, racist systems and the entrenchment of white supremacy, and the signatories committed "to hold ourselves accountable for dismantling systemic racism and promoting racial equity and justice through our investments and work" and review their portfolio holdings in order to identify investments that reinforce systemic racism, and to either engage with or divest from those companies.[25]

Impact Ecosystems

There are a number of players involved in identifying, planning, implementing, and measuring an impact investing initiative. One way to understand the process is to follow the "impact capital chain" described by Godeke and Briaud.[26] The chain begins with the asset owner, the party that holds the capital and is responsible for deciding on an investment orientation that will ultimately drive how the capital is allocated along the chain. There are a wide range of asset owners, each with their own perspectives, including retail investors, institutional endowments, private

---

[24] Saldinger, A. May 18, 2020. "Impact investing and COVID-19: A Moment for Growth or a Flight from Risk." https://devex.com/news/impact-investing-and-covid-19-a-moment-for-growth-or-a-flight-from-risk-97235

[25] https://bloomberg.com/news/articles/2020-06-18/socially-responsible-managers-commit-to-investing-against-racism

[26] Godeke, S., and P. Briaud. 2020. *Impact Investing Handbook: An Implementation Guide for Practitioners*, 46–50. Rockefeller Philanthropy Advisors.

foundations, and sovereign wealth funds. The next stages of the impact capital chain are as follows:

- *Intermediaries:* Intermediaries are entities that act as a bridge between two parties in a financial transaction, such as commercial banks, investment banks, and investment funds. Two distinct types of intermediaries in the impact capital chain are "advisors," who provide advisory services to asset owners on how to deploy their assets in exchange for fees (some advisors also offer their own investment products), and "asset managers," who develop and sell products on behalf of others to meet the investment goals of asset owners.
- *Enterprises:* Enterprises are the entities, which can include nonprofits, for-profits, and hybrid structures such as benefit corporations, which actually receive the capital and are held accountable for deploying the capital in a way that fulfills any promised impact and financial return.
- *Customers/Beneficiaries:* While the enterprise receives and deploys the capital, the impact, both positive and negative, is ultimately experienced by the customers and other beneficiaries of the enterprise's activities. Enterprises may have a diverse range of beneficiaries including not only their own customers and employees but also members of the communities in which they operate and employees and communities in their supply chains. Asset owners need to establish their own chains of communications with all of these stakeholders through engagement in order for the owners to incorporate stakeholders' views into their asset allocation decisions and assess impact on their own, rather than relying solely on reports from the enterprises.

Asset owners must also be mindful of other stakeholders that provide an enabling environment for activities carried out through the impact capital chain. These include regulators from the public sector and policymakers from the nonprofit sector, each of which play a significant role in identifying the needs of beneficiaries, structuring the operations of enterprises, and defining the range of potential investment returns for impact investment projects. As noted elsewhere in this chapter, lawmakers can create tools that are exclusively within their domain, such as tax incentives, to support impact investment. At the same time, decisions by elected officials on which projects and communities to favor with their incentives will obviously influence how asset owners are able to deploy their capital. Nonprofits with long-standing and trusted relationships in their communities can assist in asset owners in completing stakeholder analysis during the due diligence process so that asset owners can set appropriate goals and performance metrics with the enterprises that will be receiving the capital. The number of accelerators and incubators operating the impact investment arena has also increased significantly, which will hopefully mitigate risk, expand the range of available investable opportunities, and improve capacity and knowledge among prospective enterprise managers.[27]

A comprehensive ecosystem of associations, conferences, research efforts, advisors, and consultants has developed around the world in response to the growing interest in impact investing.[28] For example, standardization of measurement of environmental and social impact is obviously a crucial issue and concern and efforts in that area have included the Impact Reporting and Investment Standards IRIS; (iris.thegiin.org), a catalog of generally accepted metrics that measure social, environmental, and financial performance in an effort to support transparency, credibility, and accountability in impact measurement practices; the Global Impact Investing Ratings System, explained to be a comprehensive and transparent system for assessing the social and environmental impact of developed and emerging market companies and funds with a ratings and analytics approach analogous to Morningstar investment rankings[29]; the standards developed by the Sustainability Accounting Standards Board (www.sasb.org), a US-based independent standards-setting organization for sustainability accounting standards that was incorporated in July 2011 to meet

---

[27] Id. at 50.

[28] Greene, S. October 2015. *A Short Guide to Impact Investing.* The Case Foundation, Preface.

[29] http://thenewmediagroup.co/the-global-impact-investing-ratings-system/

the needs of investors by fostering high-quality disclosure of material sustainability information; and B Impact Assessment (https://bimpact assessment.net/), a free online assessment tool powered by B Lab that allows companies to measure their impact on their workers, communities, and customers and on the environment and compare the results to their peers and prepared a customized improvement plan.[30]

Advocacy organizations for impact investing have proliferated as part of a concerted effort to promote impact investing and develop standards responsive to the concerns of the marketplace. The Principles for Responsible Investment mentioned above are a voluntary and aspirational set of investment principles developed by an international group of institutional investors, for investors, through a process convened by the UN Secretary-General that offer a menu of possible actions for incorporating ESG issues into investment practice. The organization built around the principles has become the world's leading proponent of responsible investment and works to understand the investment implications of ESG factors and to support its international network of investor signatories (over 3,000 as of 2020, up from 100 when the Principles were launched in 2006) in incorporating these factors into their investment and ownership decisions. The International Finance Corporation (IFC) adopted a Sustainability Framework in 2006 and updated the Framework as January 1, 2012, to promote sound environmental and social practices, encourage

---

[30] Other organizations that provide assistance to impact investors the Toniic Institute, a membership-based impact investing platform for exchanging knowledge and investment opportunities (https://toniic.com/); NPX, an impact fund manager that connects nonprofit organizations seeking to raise capital for long-term impact initiatives (https://npxadvisors.com/); CREO Syndicate, a platform for investors to share experiences, discuss common interests and explore investment opportunities across the global environmental, sustainability and impact marketplace (http://creosyndicate.org/); Confluence Philanthropy, an international platform focused on advancing mission-aligned investing (https://confluencephilanthropy.org/); and ImpactAssets, a facilitator of direct impact investing within donor advised funds (https://impactassets.org/). See Mac Cormac, S., J. Finfrock and B. Fox. 2019. "Impact Investing." In *The Lawyer's Corporate Social Responsibility Deskbook*, eds. A. Gutterman et al, 245–246. Chicago: American Bar Association.

transparency and accountability, and contribute to positive development impacts. The IFC's Performance Standards, which are part of the Sustainability Framework, have become globally recognized as a benchmark for environmental and social risk management in the private sector. The Sustainability Framework also includes a Policy on Environmental and Social Sustainability, which defines the IFC's commitments to environmental and social sustainability.

The GIIN, also mentioned above, calls itself the global champion of impact investing, dedicated to increasing its scale and effectiveness around the world and carries out its work through support for development of industry networks, industry events, tools, and resources for impact measurement and management, training programs for impact investors and asset managers and industry research, market data, and publications. The International Capital Market Association (icmagroup.org) is a self-regulatory organization and trade association for participants in the capital markets that has identified the role that scaling up the financing of investments that provide environmental and social benefits will have on the transition to a sustainable global economy and sought to take the lead in this effort by championing the development and implementation of the Green Bond Principles, the Social Bond Principles, and the Sustainability Bond Guidelines as the leading framework globally for issuance of green, social, and sustainability bonds. The Impact Management Project (impactmanagementproject.com) is a forum of impact management professionals from over 2,000 organizations that has been collaborating on building a consensus on how to measure, compare, manage, and report impacts on environmental and social issues.[31] The Forum for Sustainable

---

[31] The Impact Management Project is also powering SDG Impact (sdgimpact. undp.org), a UNDP flagship initiative focusing on generating and leveraging private sector capital in delivering the SDGs. Launched in September 2018, SDG Impact seeks to provide investors, businesses and others with unified standards, tools, and services required to authenticate their contributions to achieving the SDGs and to identify SDG investment opportunities in emerging economies and developing countries. For further information, see https://sdgimpact.undp. org/SDG-Impact.pdf. SDG impact measurement and reporting is also one of the issues focused on by the Social Sector Network (https://socialsectornetwork. com/).

and Responsible Investment (https://ussif.org/) refers to itself as the non-profit hub for the sustainable, responsible, and impact investment sector in the United States and provides research, consulting, policies, media, training, national conferences, and local events to members with more than $3 trillion in AUM or advisement.

Consistent with the development of voluntary standards and instruments relating to other sustainability-related topics, industry-specific organizations and initiatives have been launched to promote impact investing, measurement, and reporting in specific industries. For example, the widely recognized Leadership in Energy and Environmental Design (LEED) green building certification program was developed by the nonprofit US Green Building Council and is now used worldwide as a rating system for the design, construction, operation, and maintenance of green buildings, homes, and neighborhoods. The Forest Stewardship Council (FSC) (fsc.org) is a multistakeholder initiative focused on the promotion of environmentally sound, socially beneficial, and economically prosperous management of the world's forests and currently operates in more than 80 countries, wherever forests are present. FSC certification ensures that products come from responsibly managed forests that provide environmental, social, and economic benefits. The FSC claims to be the world's strongest certification system, in terms of global reach, robustness of certification criteria, and number of businesses involved in the system. Fairtrade International (FI) (fairtrade.net), a nonprofit multistakeholder association that seeks to change the way trade works through better prices, decent working conditions, and a fairer deal for farmers and workers in developing countries, sets the Fairtrade Standards (www.fairtrade.net/standards), which are the requirements that producers and the businesses who buy their goods have to meet for a product to be Fairtrade certified. The Fairtrade Standards ensure fairer terms of trade between farmers and buyers, protect workers' rights, and provide the framework for producers to build thriving farms and organizations.[32]

---

[32] For further discussion, see Gutterman, A. 2020. *Sustainability Standards and Instruments*. New York, NY: Business Expert Press.

Who Are Impact Investors?

It is common to classify impact investors by how they balance impact and financial returns when constructing and executing their investment strategies. For example, Mac Cormac et al. noted that there are three classes of impact investor[33]:

- "Impact-First" or "Impact-Only" investors, typically charitable foundations, who prioritize impact over financial returns either relatively or absolutely (also known as "concessionary capital")
- "Impact and Return" investors who place approximately equal priority on impact and financial returns
- "Return-First" investors who are focused primarily on market rate financial returns but seek impact as an ancillary benefit of their investments

They pointed that an investor may allocate funds among multiple vehicles falling into different classes, such as when an investor forms and operates both a for-profit investment vehicle and a nonprofit foundation that pursue the same mission but with different levels of return risk.

According to the GIIN, impact investing has attracted a wide variety of investors, both individual and institutional, including fund managers, pension funds/insurance companies, development finance institutions (DFIs), banks and diversified financial institutions, foundations, family offices, individual investors, NGOs, and religious institutions.[34] The GIIN's 2019 Annual Impact Survey, which collected and analyzed information from 266 respondents on impact investment activities and perspectives on industry development, found that two-thirds of the respondents identified as fund managers; a majority of respondents were

[33] Mac Cormac, S., J. Finfrock, and B. Fox. 2019. "Impact Investing." In *The Lawyer's Corporate Social Responsibility Deskbook*, ed. A. Gutterman et al. 233–234. Chicago: American Bar Association.

[34] Impact Investing: A Guide to this Dynamic Market. 2019. Global Impact Investment Network, 4.

headquartered in developed markets, most commonly the United States and Canada (45 percent) and Western Europe (27 percent); two-thirds of respondents made only impact investments and the remaining third also made conventional investments; about two-thirds of respondents principally targeted market-rate returns and remaining third were split between those targeting returns closer to market rate and those targeting returns closer to capital preservation; 56 percent of respondents targeted both social and environmental impact objectives, 36 percent targeted only social objectives, and 7 percent targeted only environmental objectives; and that respondents allocated capital globally with about half of the total assets allocated to emerging markets and the other half to developed markets.[35]

Impact investors enter the marketplace from a number of different paths and each come with their own unique set of motivations and goals with respect to financial return and environmental and social impact. Financial goals are realized through the use of traditional investment criteria such as risk, diversification, liquidity, and the time horizon that meet the particular needs of the investor and, in some cases, the investor's donors or clients. Impact goals are the new piece of the puzzle for impact investors and may be based on a variety of factors such as heritage, family, faith, legacy, or experience.[36] According to Godeke and Briaud, common reasons for pursuing impact investment include engaged ownership through alignment of all of the investor's assets with the personal values or organizational mission of the investor with respect to social and environmental impact; addressing the root causes of environmental and social problems; reconfiguring and reinventing the entire economic system including shifting corporate behavior, changing the incentives of financial managers and CEOs or adding regulation to drive corporate responsibility; and advancing a particular cause by focusing investing on a specific place (e.g., community-based foundations supporting local causes and projects), people (e.g., support for projects that specifically take into

---

[35] Annual Impact Investor Survey 2019 (Global Impact Investment Network, 2019), XIXII.

[36] Godeke, S., and P. Briaud. 2020. *Impact Investing Handbook: An Implementation Guide for Practitioners*, 60. Rockefeller Philanthropy Advisors.

consideration ethnicity, race, age and/or income), or institution/institutional type (e.g., startups, community colleges, nonprofits etc.).[37]

Mac Cormac et al. noted several important trends in the impact investment sector as it entered the 2020s. First, foundations are allocating larger portions of their endowments to impact investing and shifting their investment strategies to include greater emphasis on making program-related impact investments. In some cases, nonprofits are establishing their own wholly owned investment funds to invest only in projects that further the nonprofit's tax-exempt purpose. Second, investment managers overseeing the assets for wealthy individuals and families, so-called family offices, are no longer relying strictly on the use of private foundations, which are restricted in the way that assets can be invested due to tax considerations, and are instead creating impact-first fund structures (or investing in impact-first fund structures managed by others). Third, there is growing interest in the use of "hybrid funds," which are funded by both for-profit and nonprofit investors and are often structured as an integrated combination of for-profit and nonprofit entities. Fourth, managers of for-profit funds are accommodating the interests of their investors in impact investing by establishing affiliated entities, referred to as "side cars," which focus on impact-related investment opportunities. Finally, traditional private equity investors are demonstrating more interest in impact investing.[38]

Impact investors must determine the appropriate balance between their financial and impact goals (i.e., how influential their impact goals will be in determining their investment decisions) and "impact risk," which goes to the level of uncertainty surrounding whether an investment will achieve the desired impact.[39] It is often explained that impact investors must find their place along a spectrum of intentions regarding the outcomes of their investment strategies, since intention to generate

---

[37] Id. at 60–64.

[38] Mac Cormac, S., J. Finfrock, and B. Fox, "Impact Investing." In *The Lawyer's Corporate Social Responsibility Deskbook*, eds. A. Gutterman et al., 233–234. Chicago: American Bar Association.

[39] Among the "impact risks" that impact investors should consider are evidence risk (i.e., the lack of high-quality data regarding impact), drop-off risk (i.e., the possibility that positive impacts will not endure) and unexpected impact risk, which refers to the possibility that unexpected positive or negative impacts may occur as a result of the project funded by the investor. Id. at 66.

measurable social impact alongside financial return is the defining principle of impact investing. At one extreme is traditional investing with performance measured only by financial return. At the other extreme is traditional philanthropy with performance measured by environmental and/or social impact only. Impact investors can enter the spectrum at different points between these extremes and change their strategies as they gain future experience. For example, the first steps away from "Return Only" have been characterized as a "Return First" approach and include adding an ESG screen to an existing investment (e.g., evaluating prospective investments in public companies based on ESG criteria and their commitments to corporate social responsibility) and/or committing to a thematic market-rate investment in a for-profit enterprise. The next step down the spectrum is focusing intention on impact ahead of finance through an equity investment in a benefit corporation or a local bank known for supporting community development projects, a loan to a non-profit at below-market interest rates or investing in a microfinance fund that works with entrepreneurs in developing countries.[40]

Impact investors also tend to organize their investment portfolios around impact themes and lenses. Impact themes include specific industry sectors and/or issues and examples include climate change, community development, education, energy and resources, health and wellness, social enterprises, social justice, sustainable development, and agriculture and water. Many impact investors are selecting themes that are aligned with one or more of the SDGs, such as affordable and clean energy (SDG 7).[41] Sub-themes may be used to narrow the focus within a broader topic, such as impact investors with a particular interest in early-childhood development within the larger thematic universes of education and health and wellness. An impact lens refers to a specific view or perspective that an impact investor applies when making decisions regarding

---

[40] Impact Investing: An Introduction (Rockefeller Philanthropy Advisors), 4. It is assumed that investments along the spectrum are made in "impact investees", which are described as mission-driven organizations with a market-based strategy and can include for-profits, nonprofits or hybrids.

[41] For further discussion, see Philanthropy and the SDGs: Getting Started (Rockefeller Philanthropy Advisors) and Philanthropy and the SDGs: Practical Tools for Alignment (Rockefeller Philanthropy Advisors).

the composition of the investor's impact investment portfolio. For example, an impact investor that applies a racial equity lens will focus on how a particular investment opportunity intends to impact the underlying conditions of racial equity, and gender lens investors are interested in how gender impacts all stages of the value chain including leadership and board gender balance; workforce composition and policies and practices relating to recruitment, promotion, pay equity, parental leave and flexible work, and prevention of sexual harassment; supply chains and products and services.[42] Other examples of impact lenses include climate, creative economy, diversity, inequality, and inclusiveness and refugees.[43]

According to Godeke and Briaud, the process of considering investment and impact goals and selecting the impact themes and lens that are of the greatest interest to them leads impact investor to develop their own unique "theory of change," which they described as an articulation of the intended changes for people, issues and systems arising out of the investor's asset allocation decisions. The components of a theory of change are aligned with emerging frameworks for reporting on impact investing and include the following[44]:

- *Inputs:* Inputs are the financial and nonfinancial resources that are deployed in service of a certain set of activities and

---

[42] Godeke, S. and P. Briaud. 2020. *Impact Investing Handbook: An Implementation Guide for Practitioners*, 67–68. Rockefeller Philanthropy Advisors. GIIN has described gender lens investments as investments made into companies, organizations, and funds with the explicit intent to create a positive, measurable effect on gender, and reported that about 70% of the respondents to its 2018 Annual Impact Investor Survey applied a gender lens to their investment processes and that most of them made investments into companies that had good internal gender equality policies or that targeted women and girls as beneficiaries. Annual Impact Investor Survey 2019 (Global Impact Investment Network, 2019), 28.

[43] Godeke, S., and P. Briaud. 2020. *Impact Investing Handbook: An Implementation Guide for Practitioners*. Rockefeller Philanthropy Advisors; 67.

[44] Id. at 76 (including Exhibit 3–11, a Logic Model Overview adapted from Logic Model of Measuring Impact, Impact Management Working Group of the G8 Social Impact Investment Taskforce, 2014).

may include the amount and type of capital (and the form of instrument through which that capital is provided), networks, time, and passion.

- *Activities:* Activities include the actions that are performed in support of specific impact goals and objectives such as the delivery of products and services.
- *Outputs:* Outputs are the immediate and direct tangible practices, products and services that result from the activities undertaken using the inputs and include what is delivered, to whom, when and how. Examples of outputs include the number of products or units that are sold, the number of users that are reached and information on the demographic characteristics of the direct beneficiaries of the activities.
- *Outcomes:* Outcomes are the short-term and medium-term changes, or effects, on individuals, groups, or issues (e.g., the environment) that are directly or indirectly related to the outputs from the activities undertaken using the inputs. Examples of outcomes include demonstrable improvements in the targeted health behaviors of individuals or groups or reduction in household-level economic poverty in the community in which the activities have been conducted.
- *Impacts:* Impacts are the long-term changes, or effects, achieved for populations, issues or systems due to the outcomes that have been achieved. Examples of impacts include shifts in behaviors or patterns for multiple population groups or reduction in poverty levels at the regional or national levels. When feasible, the nature of the contribution from investments relative to other inputs and influential factors should be specified.
- *Assumptions:* Assumptions include a description of what the investor believes to be true regarding the context in which the activities are conducted and the outcomes and impacts are being pursued and should be based on evidence and/or actual experience and take into account other influential inputs and factors across the various levels mentioned above.

It has been suggested that participants in the impact investment market do so, at least partially, to cope with what has been referred to as the "philanthropic paradox," meaning that investors engage in philanthropy and impact investment as a way to address and solve problems that they may have created during the course of the activities that led to their accumulation of wealth. For example, the Sackler family, which includes the founders and owners of the Purdue Pharma, a pharmaceutical company that has been widely criticized and sued for its role in the overprescription of drugs such as Oxycontin that has contributed to the North American opioid crisis, has given generous philanthropic gifts to leading institutions such as Yale University, the Guggenheim Museum, and the Serpentine Gallery to the Royal Academy in Britain. The Rockefeller family has used the wealth created from oil producing, transporting, refining, and marketing to combat the adverse impacts of these activities in the form of climate change.[45] While such efforts are certainly laudable and have often contributed to improving the lives of large numbers of people, critics continue to question how much praise should be given while progress on reducing and eventually eliminating the harm from operational activities remains slow and dismiss gaudy donations to museums and other institutions accessible to a small privileged group as "reputation laundering". Moreover, it is reasonable to expect that the Sacklers focus their wealth transfers on initiatives more closely connected to the harm they have caused, such as drug rehabilitation centers.

Another way to look at impact investing is as a means for bringing together the tools and disciplines of investment, philanthropy, and policy to generate more environmental and social benefits than would be created if these individual tools were not combined. Each of the nonprofit, public and private sector enterprises have their own unique structural characteristics, processes, and accountabilities that must be taken into account and which make collaboration problematic in many instances. For example, nonprofits depend on their donors for support; however, those donors may not have the same incentives as the persons and groups that are the intended beneficiaries of the organization's activities (i.e., the

---

[45] Godeke, S., and P. Briaud. 2020. *Impact Investing Handbook: An Implementation Guide for Practitioners*, 25. Rockefeller Philanthropy Advisors.

stakeholders). Public agencies and officials must act in accordance with agendas and budgets established by elected officials who are responding to the sentiments of voters, which often makes working with the private sector difficult. Private companies have traditionally been built and operated to achieve profit maximization for the benefit of their shareholders and have often escaped responsibility for the negative externalities of their activities. Impact investing, properly structured, draws on the specific strengths from each of the three sectors and combines them effectively to create environmental and social benefits utilizing the distinct institutional elements of each sector. One example offered by Godeke and Briaud was an impact investment project to address a need initially identified in the public sector: affordable housing. In order to effectively achieve the social benefits from the project, the public sector contributed policy tools such as tax incentives, the nonprofit sector provided the experienced gained from developing similar projects (including its skills and competencies in engaging with the beneficiaries of the project in the local community), and the commercial investors from the private sector established the goals and performance metrics to ensure that the project was completed on a timely basis and designed to fulfill both social and investment objectives.[46]

According to the Survey, respondents made over 13,000 deals in 2018 and planned to make more than 15,000 deals in 2019. The average deal size in 2018 was $2.6 million and most of the investment activity as a percentage of AUM fell into one of three categories in the following order: growth-stage companies, mature, publicly traded companies, and mature private companies. The Survey noted that while less capital was invested in venture and seed/startup stage companies, this could likely be attributed to the fact that such companies require less capital and did not necessarily reflect a lack of interest in such companies among investors. In fact, more than half of the respondents had invested in venture-stage startups and 35 percent of the respondents had supported seed/startup stage companies.[47] In general, the survey respondents seem satisfied with

---

[46] Id. at 37–38.

[47] Annual Impact Investor Survey 2019. 2019. Global Impact Investment Network, 11 and 25.

the performance of their investments, reporting that it was in line with both financial and impact expectations, and indicated a commitment to developing the impact investment industry through various contributions including sharing best practices for impact measurement and management, supporting the development of businesses focused on impact, training finance professionals, and implementing policies and practices that advanced representation in the investment process of a range of stakeholders in addition to shareholders.[48]

Not surprisingly, a significant percentage of the respondents to the GIIN's 2019 Annual Impact Survey reported that impact measurement and management were central to their goals and practices, which are defined by investors' deliberate pursuit of positive, measureable social or environmental impact. Eighty percent of the respondents indicated that desire to work for a mission-driven organization motivates their staff, and 79 percent indicated that their staff members are interested in aligning their careers with their personal values. At the organizational level, more than 80 percent of the respondents confirmed that they made impact investments because they were part of their commitment as responsible investors and intentionally pursuing impact was central to their mission. The GIIN has observed that impact investing challenges the long-held views that environmental and social issues should be addressed only by philanthropic donations and government aid, and that market investment should focus exclusively on achieving financial returns. The diverse and viable opportunities for both impact and financial return in the emerging and evolving impact investment marketplace have been a catalyst for motivating investors to participate. Examples provided by the GIIN include the following: banks, pension funds, financial advisors, and wealth managers have been able to provide new investment opportunities to both individual and institutional clients with an interest in general or specific environmental and/or social causes; Institutional investors, family offices, and foundations can leverage significantly greater assets in the impact investing marketplace to accelerate advancement of their core environmental and/or social goals, while maintaining or growing their

---

[48] Id. at XIXII.

overall endowment; and governmental entities acting as investors and DFIs can provide proof of financial viability for private-sector investors while targeting specific social and environmental goals.[49]

Impact measurement is key to the viability and progress of the impact investment market and the respondents to the GIIN's 2019 Annual Impact Survey reported that impact measurement was almost universally practiced and that they typically relied on a mix of qualitative information, proprietary metrics, and metrics aligned to IRIS or other standard frameworks.[50] One particularly interesting finding from the survey was that more than 60 percent of investors specifically tracked their investment performance to impact themes aligned to the SDGs, the most common ones being decent work and economic growth, no poverty, reduced inequalities, and good health and well-being. Aligning performance measurement with the SDGs is consistent with the overall profile of investors' motivations for making impact investments since over half of the respondents to the survey indicated that they saw impact investing as a good path to contributing to the global agenda on environmental and social responsibility that included the SDGs.

Considerations for Recipients of Impact Investment

Companies now operate in an environment in which more and more capital providers are taking sustainability issues into consideration when deciding whether to fund a particular company or project and this means that the entire board of directors needs to understand how the company's ESG-related strategies, principles, and practices can impact the company's access to capital and the stability of its relationship with investors and bankers. An additional consideration is measurement and reporting of ESG-related performance, a topic that must be consider by several board-level committees such as the audit, finance, disclosure, and corporate social responsibility committees. Measurement and reporting techniques

---

[49] Impact Investing: A Guide to this Dynamic Market, 5. Global Impact Investment Network.

[50] Annual Impact Investor Survey 2019. 2019. Global Impact Investment Network, XIV.

are evolving and differ across jurisdictions; however, there are emerging standards that need to be understood as more investors and lenders rely on sustainability and ESG reporting for collecting information necessary for them to make decisions about allocating their capital.

When reviewing and approving the company's financial strategies and specific capital projects board members need to be mindful of the various factors that motivate investors and decision makers to incorporate sustainability aspects into their investment and lending decisions[51]:

- Many investors and lenders take sustainability issues into consideration in order to make better risk management decisions, avoid future financial issues and make better long-term investment and lending decisions. Investors and lenders are increasingly skittish about funding companies and projects that carry high legal and reputational risks due to concerns about compliance with applicable laws and regulations and ESG norms and standards.

- A growing number of investors and lenders are focusing on sustainability as a means for uncovering promising new business opportunities and undervalued assets. Companies that can offer investors and lenders a path to participate in financing innovative solutions to environmental and/or social problems can tap into new pools of capital.

- Investors are taking a more values-driven approach to funding decisions and avoiding investment in companies or projects considered to be "unethical" and/or which are likely to cause environmental or social harm. At that same time, these investors are proactively seeking out projects that have a demonstrable positive environmental or social impact.

- Certain investors, as well as shareholder activists, are interested in applying pressure on companies to change their behavior with respect to operational activities that have adverse environmental and social impacts (e.g., threatening

[51] Krauss, A., P. Kruger and J. Meyer. September 2016. *Sustainable Finance in Switzerland: Where Do We Stand?* 16. Zurich: Sustainable Finance Institute.

to withhold or withdraw capital unless companies cease to engage in activities considered to be unsustainable).

- Some investors, like consumers, enjoy being associated with "good causes" and are therefore driven to invest in companies that have a good reputation with respect to ESG matters as a means for embellishing their own social identity.

For lenders, as opposed to investors seeking attractive risk-adjusted returns in addition to recovery of their original capital, ESG issues appear in their reluctance to enter into loan transactions that might ultimately involve them in financing controversial activities and/or projects that are overexposed to identifiable environmental or social risks and potential liabilities. Lenders are not only concerned about the possibility that ESG issues for the parties to whom they lend may impact their ability to repay but also fear reputational damage from being associated with such borrowers and their environmentally harmful and/or unethical practices. Many lenders follow an approach similar to the negative/exclusionary screening described above.[52] At the same time, however, lenders are themselves interested in enhancing their sustainability reputations and are adopting various types of positive screening and ESG integration methodologies into their loan analysis and proactively seeking qualified borrowers in the areas of interest to thematic sustainability investors.

Directors need to understand the role that investors and lenders can play in impacting the future structure of the economy and, in turn, the influence that the priorities of investors and lenders can have on the business and financial strategies of their potential portfolio companies. This means making various adjustments to the how the board approaches some of its traditional duties and responsibilities. For example, companies are being urged to move beyond conventional net present value analysis of projects to implement sustainable asset valuation and capital budgeting techniques such as analyzing projects based on "net present sustainable value," which has been described as estimating "the net present value added across financial, environmental and social dimensions

---

[52] Krauss, A., P. Kruger and J. Meyer. September 2016. *Sustainable Finance in Switzerland: Where Do We Stand?* 20. Zurich: Sustainable Finance Institute.

using a required rate of return that considers not only investors' opportunity cost for their financial capital, but also the opportunity costs of the environmental and social capital inputs."[53] With respect to capital budgeting, analysts are beginning to favor in incremental savings of water, energy, and waste.

Another transition necessary for companies to take advantage of sustainable financing opportunities is shifting toward reporting and disclosure that includes ESG matters, particularly when companies are seeking targeted financing for projects based on renewable energy, climate change action, community, and economic development and natural resource conservation and management. Oversight of insurance matters by the board must take into consideration the evolving needs of insurance companies to mitigate their exposure to sustainability-related risks (e.g., natural disasters, ecosystem, and community damage from operational activities and litigation costs associated with claims from employees based on hazardous work conditions and/or consumers based on issues with defective and/or hazardous products).

The Future of Impact Investing

As for the overall state of the impact investing market, the respondents to the GIIN's 2019 Annual Impact Survey noted that significant progress had been made over the prior year with respect to research on market activity, trends, performance, and practice, as well as in the sophistication of impact measurement and management practice and the availability of professionals with relevant skill sets. However, the respondents expressed concerns about several challenges to further progress such as a lack of appropriate capital across the risk/return spectrum, a lack of high-quality investment opportunities with track records and a lack of suitable exit options.[54] A Case Foundation publication issued in October 2015 suggested that growth of impact investing required additional work on a robust pipeline of investable deals, better data on business and fund

---

[53] Ignited, A Brief Overview of Sustainable Finance, https://ignited.global/publications/crimson-financier/brief-overview-sustainable-finance
[54] Id. at 6.

performance, expanded opportunities for exits and the return of capital, actionable research on impacts and outcomes, and more products and easier "on ramps" for investors to get started.[55]

Ideas for the path forward for the continued development of the impact investing market and ecosystem have been collected in the GIIN's *Roadmap for the Future of Impact Investing: Reshaping Financing Markets*, which was produced by roughly 350 stakeholders engaged by GIIN in order to suggest both a vision for more inclusive and sustainable financial markets and articulate a plan for the future progress of impact investing. The *Roadmap* details the following six categories of action to drive progress toward the vision[56]:

- Strengthen the identity of impact investing by establishing clear principles and standards for impact investing and sharing best practices for impact measurement, management, and reporting
- Change the paradigm that governs investment behavior and expectations about the responsibility of finance in society via asset owner leadership, alignment of incentives with impact and updated fundamental investment theory
- Design tools and services that support the incorporation of impact into the routine analysis, allocation, and deal-making activities of investors (e.g., develop ratings for impact and build analysis and allocation tools that incorporate risk, return and impact)
- Develop products suited to the needs and preferences of the full spectrum of investors, from retail to institutional and of various types of investees, commit capital to emerging fund managers, and advance blended-finance vehicles

---

[55] Greene, S. October 2015. *A Short Guide to Impact Investing.* The Case Foundation, Preface.

[56] https://thegiin.org/research/publication/giin-roadmap (as modified from additional descriptions appearing in Highlights from Roadmap for the Future of Impact Investing: Reshaping Financial Markets (Global Impact Investment Network, 2020)).

- Increase supply of trained investment professionals and
  pipeline of investment-ready enterprises focused on impact
  through targeted professional education (both graduate
  education and professional training and certification) for both
  finance professionals and business managers
- Introduce policies and regulation that both remove barriers
  and incentivize impact investments including clarify fiduciary
  duty, establish tax incentives for impact investments and
  create an environment conductive to impact investing

The *Roadmap* categories were developed to emphasize three priorities
that must be addressed in order for the impact investing industry to continue to grow: prove feasibility at scale (i.e., demonstrate progress against
environmental and social challenges and the ability to generate satisfactory financial returns for investors across a range of risk-return appetites);
increase accessibility of impact investments to a much broader set of individuals and institutions; and provide greater clarity and standardization
among impact investors with myriad motivations, return expectations
and approaches to achieving and measuring impact.[57]

The GIIN's 2019 Annual Impact Survey provided more details on
the steps that participants in the impact investing market believed should
be taken with respect to several of the *Roadmap* categories. For example, a significant percentage of the respondents called on governments
to advance the impact investing market through creation of tax or other
incentives for impact investors and social enterprises, support for capacity
building for investors, direct impact investing and impact-conscious government procurement, and amendments to governance frameworks to
explicitly include impact considerations in fiduciary duties and support
for educational programs for new market participants. Respondents also
reported on significant legal and regulatory barriers and challenges that
need to be addressed including regulations on foreign investment and
ownership; inconsistent and unpredictable application of policies, particularly relating to foreign direct investment and taxes; complex capital

---

[57] Id.

controls; interest rate caps; restrictive application and/or interpretation of fiduciary duties and nonexistent or limited regulation of impact investing and related reporting.[58]

Governments have been responding to calls for them to increase their support for impact investing through the development of new regulatory frameworks and policies to encourage private impact investing and the formation of impactful business enterprises. Examples of such actions highlighted in GIIN's 2019 Annual Impact Survey included the French Impact Initiative launched by the French Government in January 2019 to unite and diversify social entrepreneurs and create a national social innovation accelerator to mobilize EUR 1 billion of public and private funding in five years for venture- and growth-stage businesses and provide them with capacity building support to scale; the creation of a Fund for Social Innovation by the Portuguese government to provide equity and debt financing for enterprises recognized as innovation and social entrepreneurship initiatives; the designation of "opportunity zones" by the US federal government to encourage and facilitate investments in economically distressed areas; and the announcement by the Office of Social Impact Investment of the state government of New South Wales in Australia of an initiative to finance innovate strategies to prevent homelessness among people exiting government services such as public housing or juvenile justice. The Development Working Group, a subgroup of the G20, has issued the "G20 Call on Financing for Inclusive Businesses," a declaration that calls on governments to provide friendly regulatory environments for inclusive businesses in order to promote sustainable development.[59]

Case studies and other illustrations and explanations of the application of the principles and guidelines include in this publication are available from a variety of sources prepared and published by organizations with substantial experience relating to impact investing including Rockefeller Philanthropy Advisors and the GIIN. Among the topics covered in these case studies are articulating mission and values and defining impact,

---

[58] Annual Impact Investor Survey 2019. 2019. Global Impact Investment Network, 40.

[59] Id. at 41.

implementation tools and tactics, developing an impact investment policy, building the pipeline and generating deal flow, analyzing deals, evaluating impact, impact investing governance, organizing for impact, and investment advisory committees.[60] The Annual Impact Investor Surveys published by the GIIN also provide insights into developments in the impact investment market, such as growing interest in gender lens investing, investing in refugee issues, human resources, diversity and inclusion, and the role of governments and policy.[61]

---

[60] See, e.g., Godeke, S., and D. Bauer. 2008. *Mission-Related Investing: A Policy and Implementation Guide for Foundation Trustees*. Rockefeller Philanthropy Advisors and Godeke, S., and R. Pomares. August 2010. *Solutions for Impact Investors: From Strategy to Implementation*. Rockefeller Philanthropy Advisors; Godeke, S., and P. Briaud. 2020. *Impact Investing Handbook: An Implementation Guide for Practitioners*. Rockefeller Philanthropy Advisors and the Annual Impact Investor Survey 2019. 2019. Global Impact Investment Network.

[61] Annual Impact Investor Survey 2019. 2019. Global Impact Investment Network, 40.

CHAPTER 3

Impact Investment Tools, Structures, and Instruments

Impact investors pursue their investment and impact goals through the decisions they make regarding the impact investing products that will be included in their portfolios. These decisions should be guided by the investor's governance documents (i.e., the impact investment statement and impact policy statement) and products may be selected from among a range of asset classes including the following[1]:

- *Cash:* Cash is a low-risk and highly liquid asset class that can be deployed into impact vehicles, such as certificates of deposits in community banks, Green Bank deposits, linked deposit/guarantees with community development financial institutions, or short-term loan funds to social enterprises. Guarantees are a good way for private foundations to leverage their endowment to support social enterprises by enabling those enterprises to gain access to capital by lowering the risks to its market-rate investors.[2]
- *Fixed Income:* Fixed income assets provide a fixed stream of income that is established when the investment is made and continues until the agreed maturity date when the principal is repaid. Impact investors can choose from among a

---

[1] Godeke, S., and P. Briaud. 2020. *Impact Investing Handbook: An Implementation Guide for Practitioners*. Rockefeller Philanthropy Advisors, 110.

[2] Godeke, S., and D. Bauer. 2008. *Mission-Related Investing: A Policy and Implementation Guide for Foundation Trustees*, 63–64. Rockefeller Philanthropy Advisors.

growing array of debt instruments designed to raise capital for impact-related activities such as municipal and corporate bonds that focus on targeting specific locations or activities, green bonds, social enterprise credit, global development bonds, and social growth municipal bonds.

- *Public Equity:* Public equity refers to shares of stock and other instruments (e.g., actively managed sustainability funds and exchange-traded funds) traded on recognized and regulated securities exchanges that provide impact investors with liquidity, access to ESG data through mandated disclosure requirements, and opportunities to engage with management. Decisions on public equities for impact investing are generally based on screening, ESG integration, and thematic preferences. Data indicates that interest in public equity impact strategies has surged over the last few years bringing large numbers of retail and institutional investors into the marketplace and fueling demand for better ESG data disclosures and ESG performance measurement tools.[3]

- *Hedge Funds:* Hedge funds and other alternative investments use pooled funds that employ different strategies to earn active return for their investors including aggressive tactics such as derivatives and leverage. Hedge fund managers have been slow to adopt impact investing and since hedge funds are less regulated than mutual funds and other investment vehicles they may be less transparent regarding their holdings and strategies. However, there is evidence that hedge fund participation in impact investing is growing, primarily at the "overlay-manager level" as hedge fund managers incorporate Socially Responsible Investing and ESG-labeled funds in their

---

[3] Kamphuis, M., and M. Meulemans. November 2018. "How to Maximise Impact When Investing in Public Equities: A Practical Guide to Get Started with Building an Impactful Public Equities Portfolio." file:///C:/Users/Alan/Downloads/how-to-maximise-impact-when-investing-in-public-equities-nov-2018.pdf

client portfolios.[4] Hedge funds also participate in blended debt/equity hybrid structures to support thematic impact projects and enterprises.[5]

- *Private Equity:* Private equity and other early-stage investments, particularly venture capital, can create impact through supporting innovative and high-growth business models in specific impact themes (e.g., community development, clean tech and energy, water technology, and ed tech) and investors may use board seats to direct impact-integrated corporate strategies and provide entrepreneurs/promoters with management support and access to other resources necessary for the enterprise to be successful. Pressure is growing on fund managers to mitigate risks to their finances and reputation by incorporating environmental and social issues in their investment decisions and building a sustainable portfolio, particularly as concern about ESG increases within the investment community and evidence that environmental and social impact improves financial returns continues to grow.[6]

- *Real Estate:* Real estate investments can create impact through their environmental footprint (e.g., Green Real Estate projects developed based on sustainability principles to deliver a real, physical asset that outperforms today's building standards for

---

[4] In May 2017, the Principles for Responsible Investment ("PRI") launched of the first industry-standard due diligence questionnaire ("DDQ") for hedge funds to focus on responsible investments. The PRI explained that the tool, a standardized set of questions, was intended to assist investors in their managers' selection and assessment process and make it easier for them to identify those fund managers who have the staff, knowledge and structure in place to incorporate ESG factors in the investment decision-making process. https://unpri.org/hedge-funds/responsible-investment-ddq-for-hedge-funds/125.article

[5] Impact Investing: A Sustainable Strategy for Hedge Funds (November 22, 2016), https://valuewalk.com/2016/11/impact-investing-sustainable-strategy-hedge-funds/

[6] Yang, K., U. Akhtar, J. Dessard and A. Seemann. 2019. "Private Equity Investors Embrace Impact Investing." *Bain & Company.* April 17, 2019, https://bain.com/insights/private-equity-investors-embrace-impact-investing/

energy efficiency, water efficiency, and reduced waste) as well as through the important contributions they can make to addressing social issues such as safe and affordable housing, community building, and enterprise development. Governments have moved to support investments in this asset class through the creation of opportunity zones to provide tax incentives to encourage long-term investments in low-income communities.[7]

- *Commodities and Real Assets:* Investments in commodities and real assets, such as timber and water rights, can provide targeted impact leveraging tangible resources. Impact investors have funded agriculture/food systems to promote health and wellness and been involved in ethical mining projects to support community development, sustainable feedstock projects to support renewal energy, and sustainable timber projects to promote sustainable development and agriculture.

The various asset classes can be distinguished based on a number of factors including the asset owner's relationship to the investment (i.e., debt holders are creditors of the company while equity holders have an ownership stake in the company), the asset owner's anticipated return on the investment (i.e., debt holders expect to be paid a fixed rate of interest on their investment and to receive their principal back within an agreed time horizon while equity holders are usually not assured any fixed return and depend on the company's declaration and payment of dividends and the eventual sale of their equity stake in the company to realize a return), risk/return (i.e., cash is a low-risk/return investment while private investments and real assets come with higher risk/return), liquidity (i.e., equity and debt assets purchased in public markets are more liquid than those purchased in private markets), and time horizon (i.e., timing for return of capital must be aligned with the time required to address the specific environmental or social challenge and generate the desired non-financial outcomes).[8] The primary goal for cash investment is liquidity while the other asset classes offer investors income and wealth preservation (i.e., fixed income), capital

---

[7] http://apparealestate.com/impact/

[8] Godeke, S., and P. Briaud. 2020. *Impact Investing Handbook: An Implementation Guide for Practitioners*, 90 and 101. Rockefeller Philanthropy Advisors.

appreciation (i.e., public equity, hedge funds and private equity), and infla-tion protection (i.e., real estate, commodities and real assets).

Each investor has its own approach to prioritizing the various factors that distinguish asset classes. For example, the composition of an inves-tor's beneficiary group may dictate that investments be weighted toward instruments that offer a fixed rate of interest and promise return of capital within a specific time horizon. Other investors may have a longer time horizon that allows them to consider investments in enterprises working on environmental or social problems that will require patience regarding both impact/outcome and financial return on investment.[9] Investors may construct their portfolio by first deciding on a particular asset class that meets their needs and makes them feel comfortable in terms of available data, liquidity, and other factors, and then select investments within that class that fit with their specific impact goals and interests. For example, an impact investor acting in the public equities market might direct capital to actively managed sustainability funds if the investor is interested in climate change or may choose micro-cap listed companies if the investor is focused on social enterprise. Alternatively, impact investors may select a specific environmental or social cause and then make related investments across a range of asset classes (e.g., impact investors interested in educa-tion might invest in charter school and tax-exempt bonds, hedge funds pursuing tuition financing strategies, private equity funds investing in ed tech and education delivery projects and enterprises, and School Green Building and Charter Facilities Finance).[10] Choices among the various

---

[9] Traditionally many foundations had long time horizons for their investment activities given that their governing documents provided for perpetual existence; however, in recent years there has been a trend toward "spending down", which is a requirement that all funds made available for investment must be spent within a specified time period. The byproduct of this trend is that foundations are more motivated to select investments that will have significant impact in a shorter period of time and fulfill the need for liquidity and exit in order to sunset the fund by the end of the time horizon. Id. at 103 (including discussion of key investment considerations for executing a "spending down" strategy) and 104 (case study of the use of "spending down" by The Grove Foundation in its impact investment strategy).

[10] Godeke, S., and P. Briaud. 2020. *Impact Investing Handbook: An Implementa-tion Guide for Practitioners*, 113. Rockefeller Philanthropy Advisors.

asset classes are obviously important for many reasons; however, they are particularly relevant to the selection of investment managers and advisors, all of whom must have appropriate experience with the tools necessary to make decisions among opportunities in the specific asset classes, and the design of the incentive structures for those managers and advisors.

Impact Tools

Impact tools are actions that impact investors can take in order to effectively apply their theory of change, as explained in the previous chapter, to create a portfolio that is aligned with the investor's investment and impact goals. Surveys of global money managers and other research have identified the following commonly used impact tools[11]:

- *Engagement/active ownership:* Engagement/active ownership is the identification of material factors where investors can use their powers as shareholders or debt holders to influence corporate behavior through direct corporate engagement, such as communicating with senior management and/or directors of companies, taking a seat on the board of directors, filing or co-filing shareholder proposals for actions at shareholder meetings and proxy voting that is directed by ESG guidelines. To be effective, this tool should be used to demonstrate long-term commitment by the investor and a desire to collaborate with management to influence corporate change. Since a single investor often does not have enough voting power to introduce a shareholder proposal on its own, consideration should be given to joining shareholder coalitions that have emerged around specific issues such as climate change (e.g., Coalition for

---

[11] Adapted from Godeke, S., and P. Briaud. 2020. *Impact Investing Handbook: An Implementation Guide for Practitioners,* 92–101. Rockefeller Philanthropy Advisors, (citing Amel-Zadeh, A., and G. Serafeim. 2018. "Why and How Investors use ESG Information: Evidence from a Global Survey." *Financial Analysts Journal* 74, no. 3, CFA Institute, p. 87).

Environmentally Responsible Economies, or "Ceres") in order to have greater impact.

- *Negative screening:* Negative screening is the exclusion of certain sectors (e.g., private prisons, tobacco, or contraception), companies or practices from a fund or portfolio on the basis of specific ESG criteria.

- *Positive screening:* Positive screening is the inclusion of certain sectors, companies, or practices in a fund or portfolio on the basis of specific minimum ESG criteria. When using this tool it is important to realize that many of the projects and initiatives that would "qualify" are in riskier sectors due to the untested nature of underlying technologies and methods (e.g., renewable energy) and a pool of enterprises skewed toward early-stage ventures.

- *Full integration of ESG factors into financial analysis:* Full integration into individual stock valuation is the systematic and explicit inclusion of ESG factors into traditional financial analysis and selection of individual stocks (e.g., as inputs into cash-flow forecasts and/or cost-of-capital estimates). Among other things, investors take into account ESG policies, performances, practices, and impact, relying on a proliferation of data from providers offering public data, ESG rating services and niche providers specializing in specific themes such as carbon disclosures and gender equality.[12] Investors use ESG

---

[12] Investors may use different methods to describe ESG and the relevant factors for their investment decisions. For example, in one instance an investor analyzed the way in which enterprises consumed and generated four classes of capital: human (interactions with people with whom the enterprise had a direct relationship, such as employees); natural (how the enterprise makes use of natural resources and handles waste products and the enterprise's overall impact on the natural environment); civic (interactions with communities including customers, neighbors and regulators) and financial (effects of the enterprise's governance practices and capital-outlay decisions on capital providers). Id. at 98 (describing the "overall impact" or "net contribution" analysis conducted by the Heron Foundation during the construction of its investment portfolio).

integration in different ways in their investment processes: some include companies that have stronger ESG policies and practices, similar to positive screening, while others exclude or avoid companies with poor ESG track records in the same way that companies may be excluded through negative screening.

- *Relative/best-in-class screening:* Relative/best-in-class screening is the investment in sectors, companies, or projects selected based on their ESG performance relative to industry peers and is a tool that is often used to distinguish among larger global corporations with readily identifiable competition.

- *Overlay/portfolio tilt:* Overlay/portfolio tilt is the use of certain investment strategies or products to change specific aggregate ESG characteristics of a fund or investment portfolio to a desired level, such as by aligning an investment portfolio toward a desired carbon footprint.

- *Thematic investment:* Thematic investment drives the creation or expansion of specific outcomes by focusing on investment in themes or assets specifically related to ESG factors, such as clean energy, green technology, or sustainable agriculture. Many thematic investments are made in individual projects or early-stage enterprises (e.g., an early-stage educational-technology company) because it is easier to demonstrate outcomes in those asset classes and investors are able to exercise more direct control over those types of investments.

- *Risk factor/risk premium investing:* Risk factor/risk premium investing is the inclusion of ESG information in the analysis of systematic risks (e.g., factor-investment strategies such as "Smart Beta").[13]

- *Catalytic concessionary capital:* Catalytic concessionary investing seeks to generate ("catalyze") positive impact by having

---

[13] Hanke, B., G. Quigley, and A. Cain. 2016. "How Smart is Factor Investing and Smart Beta: Which Factors Matter most and Why Choose Factor Investing at All?", June 13, 2016, https://london.edu/think/how-smart-is-factor-investing-and-smart-beta

investors agree to accept certain subsidies or concessions (e.g., disproportionate risk and/or concessionary returns relative to investment made with the expectation of traditional risk-adjusted market-rate returns) in order to deploy investments that would not have otherwise occurred.[14]

Impact investors may use one or more of the impact tools mentioned above at the same time and generally will combine several of the tools in order to make better decisions about the design of their portfolios, influence the actions of the investees (and intermediaries, if any), and track portfolio performance. For example, screening, both negative and positive, has long been used by investors to make threshold decisions regarding which types of companies and/or sectors should be included or excluded when creating a portfolio that is aligned with their values, even though the link between screening and contribution is not as clear as with some of the other impact tools; however, screening alone is no substitute for the application of additional criteria such as financial performance, management quality, and ESG integration. The desire to create or expand

---

[14] Common subsidies and concessions used in catalytic capital include accepting an expected rate of return that is below market relative to the expected risk; providing credit enhancement for a project in the form of a guarantee, which allows the impact investor to support a project without initially deploying capital (capital would only be required if the company defaults on its obligations to other investors); taking a subordinated/junior position vis-à-vis other creditors or equity holders, such as subordinating repayment of a loan to the preference of a senior commercial lender providing larger amounts of capital; accepting a longer, or less certain, time horizon for repayment of capital than other commercial investors in the project; and agreeing to non-traditional/non-market terms such as no collateral, smaller investment size or flexible use of proceeds, concessions that may be appropriate for projects that will require additional research and development before they would be attractive to other commercial investors. Godeke, S., and P. Briaud. 2020. *Impact Investing Handbook: An Implementation Guide for Practitioners*, 99. Rockefeller Philanthropy Advisors, (noting that Debra Schwartz of the MacArthur Foundation first described these concessions as the 5Ps (price, pledge, position, patience and purpose) in 2013). See also Brest, P., and K. Born. Fall 2013. "Unpacking the Impact in Impact Investing." *Stanford Social Innovation Review*, 22.

specific outcomes while focusing on a particular impact problem leads to the use of thematic investing among opportunities that survive the screening process and decisions among those opportunities will rely on the data and methodologies used for ESG integration. Once a project or portfolio company is selected the investor can use engagement/active ownership to influence the managers of the project or company and the tools of ESG integration to measure and analyze financial and impact performance. In addition, investors can require the use of one of the impact transaction structures discussed elsewhere in this chapter, such as "pay-for-success" or impact covenants, to keep projects and companies focused on impact targets.

Impact Structures

Each impact investment needs to be structured properly to optimize impact while fitting within the investor's overarching impact investment goals and policies. Impact structures are a function of decisions made regarding the investor, intermediary and enterprise vehicles, and the use of certain transactional tools (e.g., "pay-for-success," "responsible exits," and covenants) that are intended to drive specific impact outcomes. Not every structure uses each of the three elements; for example, individual asset owners may invest directly in social enterprises without using an intermediary. The ability of asset owners to influence the structures, governance, and purposes of intermediaries and enterprises will also vary depending on the circumstances, such as the amount and type of capital that the asset owner is willing to provide and the degree to which the asset owner is willing and able to be actively engaged with the activities of the entity that receives the funds. For example, there is a significant difference in the potential influence between an investment in a public company through a limited partnership intermediary and making a direct investment in a startup targeting a specific environmental or social problem that includes the opportunities to serve on the startup's board of directors.

Asset owners can choose from among a variety of legal structures to conduct their impact investing activities based on their individual preferences regarding factors such as tax benefits, expenses, anonymity, and flexibility.[15] Traditionally asset owners separated their financial investments and philanthropic activities into two different entities: partnerships and holding companies for financial investments and public charities, private foundations and community foundations for philanthropy. Impact investing, to the extent it existed, was generally carried out through one of the philanthropic vehicles, which by law provided tax benefits for investments that fell within classes of "exempt purposes" under the Internal Revenue Code including initiatives that addressed social issues such as education, literacy, relief of the poor or underprivileged, lessening neighborhood tensions, eliminating prejudice, and discrimination and improving the quality of life in communities. However, to avail itself of the advantages of a foundation, particularly the potential tax benefits, asset owners need to be prepared to understand and adhere to the complex laws and regulations applicable to private foundations or public charities and make public disclosures regarding the management and activities of the foundation.[16]

For-profit businesses have often conducted most of their philanthropic and sustainability activities through a corporate foundation, which is a separate legal entity (i.e., a nonprofit corporation) that is formed by and closely affiliated with the company and which is to be organized and operated in a manner that reflects the mission and interests of the company and its stakeholders. While corporate foundations generally rely primarily, if not exclusively, on regular contributions from

---

[15] Godeke, S., and P. Briaud. 2020. *Impact Investing Handbook: An Implementation Guide for Practitioners*, 106. Rockefeller Philanthropy Advisors.

[16] For example, among other things, a private foundation must: satisfy minimum annual payout requirements of at least 5% of the fair market value of the previous year's assets; pay a 2% tax annually on net investment income; avoid self-dealing transactions with insiders; limit its ownership interest in any one business to 20% in order to avoid "excess business holdings"; avoid risky investments that jeopardize the accomplishment of the foundation's charitable purposes, which means that the foundation will need to perform rigorous due diligence before making an investment; and avoid contributions to individuals, other private foundations or non-charitable organizations which might be deemed to be "taxable expenditures".

the company to support their giving activities it is also possible for the foundation to solicit funding from public sources in order to expand the potential range of the foundation's work. Like any business, a corporate foundation decides each year how much of its assets will be currently deployed in philanthropic activities and how much will be set aside as an endowment reserved for future use.

Establishing a corporate foundation provides the company with flexibility to make its philanthropic contributions in a way that is most efficient from both a tax and overall financial perspective. For example, if the company is having a profitable year it can make a larger tax-deductible contribution to the foundation, thus reducing the company's tax bill while enhancing the resources of the foundation without straining the financial assets of the company. The contributions made during profitable years will be available in later years to support continuity in the foundation's programs even if the company itself is not doing as well in those years and thus is not able to make a current year contribution to the foundation.

Using a corporate foundation allows companies to impose stronger requirements on their donees regarding the use of grant funds and also allows company executives to direct requests for support of charitable causes to an external unit that is still aligned with the company's strategy and mission but has its own decision-making procedures. However, to avail itself of the advantages of a foundation, particularly the potential tax benefits, companies need to be prepared to understand and adhere to the complex laws and regulations applicable to private foundations or public charities and make public disclosures regarding the management and activities of the foundation.

Impact investment activities of foundations and other mission-investing organizations generally fall into two categories: mission-related investments, described as risk-adjusted, market-rate investments made as part of a foundation's endowment that have a positive social impact while contributing to the foundation's long-term financial stability and growth; and program-related investments (PRIs), which are defined in the Internal Revenue Code as below-market-rate investments made by private foundations that are designed to achieve specific program objectives consistent with the foundation's charitable purposes and which can be included as a qualified distribution in order to fulfill the foundation's 5 percent annual payout obligations.[17] PRIs are made without an expectation of a commercial return and cannot be structured to maximize returns; however, if a PRI ultimately turns out to be more financially successful than expected, it will not lose its status as a PRI under the tax laws. PRIs are often the first step for foundations looking to upgrade their financial management skills in order to eventually engage in more sophisticated impact investing structures. Among other things, a PRI program requires expertise and processes in due diligence, tracking investment performance and adherence to covenants by the investee, engagement and exit strategies. Many foundations will co-invested with other private investors with more experience. A majority of PRIs by foundations are in the form of loans; however, PRIs can also be found among other asset classes such as private equity funds, commodities such as sustainable lumber and real estate.[18]

MISSION Framework for Analyzing Program-Related Investments

In their 2018 publication titled *Mission Investing: A Framework for Family Foundations*, the Michael and Susan Dell Foundation and NYU Wagner described a MISSION Framework that charities engaged in impact investing could use to screen and analyze so-called program-related investments (PRIs), which are statutorily defined types of charitable investments that must have as their primary purpose accomplishment of one or more charitable purposes and must not have production of income or appreciation of property as one of their significant purposes. In effect, PRIs are grants are admittedly different than other types of impact investments; however, the criteria included in the MISSION Framework can be broadly applied during the due diligence process.

---

[17] Impact Investing: An Introduction (Rockefeller Philanthropy Advisors), 19. Resources for foundations and other mission-investing organizations interested in impact investing are available from Confluence Philanthropy, Investors Circle, Mission Investors Exchange, The Impact and the Forum for Sustainable and Responsible Investment. Id. at 36–37.

[18] Godeke, S., and D. Bauer. 2008. *Mission-Related Investing: A Policy and Implementation Guide for Foundation Trustees*, 61. Rockefeller Philanthropy Advisors.

- M—*Market:* Ability to create new markets, test innovative products and services, or serve new demographics through the use of patient capital and/or fund investments. Objective is to prove business model's long-term financial sustainability and demonstrated demand (i.e., product/market fit) in order to attract traditional capital and spur competition.
- I—*Impact:* Use of a PRI may induce organizational growth, programmatic scale, or similar effects that can lead to widespread, demonstrable outcomes in a relatively short time. The investee should be able to produce measurable outcomes that are clearly connected to programmatic strategies.
- S—*Scale:* Investment can scale a nascent market to serve low-income customers or move an existing market to have a higher proportion of low-income customers.
- S—*Sustainable:* Long-term financial health increases the likelihood of an investee's success and the achievement of social impact at scale. A deep understanding of organizational risk factors, operational metrics, exit path strategies, and scenario planning helps to mitigate firm-level risk. Relationships with top management and other investors, along with ongoing data collection and analysis, are additional tools for ensuring sustainability.
- I—*Incrementality:* The investment adds value and is an opportunity beyond the scope of, not a replacement of, mainstream capital.
- O—*Organization:* The entrepreneur/promoter and other capital providers need to be committed to both the market and charitable objectives of the investment and be open and supportive of the philanthropic investors' role, including board representation, reporting requirements, and operational target analysis.

- N—*Next:* The investment has a logical path to scale market sustainability through a capital strategy or recycling of capital. The inherent sustainability of the model should enable it to attract new forms of capital to allow significant scale up of the outreach and impact. There is a steadfast commitment to accountability by the investee, driven by expectations of capital recovery.

Source: *Mission Investing: A Framework for Family Foundations* (NYU Wagner and the Michael and Susan Dell Foundation) (2018) (reproduced in S. Godeke and P. Briaud, *Impact Investing Handbook: An Implementation Guide for Practitioners*) (Rockefeller Philanthropy Advisors, 2020, 102).

As time has gone by and tools for achieving both financial and impact goals have appeared and evolved, asset owners have sought greater flexibility to efficiently invest in enterprises and projects addressing social issues, leading to the growing popularity of hybrid structures combining nonprofit entities and limited liability companies (LLCs) and donor-advised funds (DAFs). The most well-known example of a hybrid structure is the Omidyar Network created by the founder of eBay and his wife to use impact investing of their significant wealth from eBay's initial public offering to make a positive contribution to the world.[19] They originally began their philanthropic activities through a traditional family foundation that made grants to worthy causes; however, they became frustrated at the difficulties in scaling impact in the nonprofit sector due to the lack of sustainable revenue models and they also noticed that there were an increasing number of social impact opportunities in the for-profit sector. Given this, they put in place a hybrid structure described as a "flexible checkbook" that makes it possible for investment to be made in both for-profit enterprises and nonprofit organizations to create sector-based

---

[19] The discussion in this paragraph is adapted from Building a Philanthropic Investment Firm: A New Approach. Omidyar Network.

change. The Omidyars, through their family trust, funded two sibling entities through annual distributions. One is a traditional tax-exempt nonprofit entity that makes grants, mission-related investments and PRIs. They found that grants are particularly well suited to providing public goods, helping disadvantaged populations and subsidizing the creation of goods and services that benefit society. The second entity is a taxable LLC, which is used to make for-profit investments in early-stage innovations that seek to create significant social impact and which have the power to provide value to their customers and the potential to become self-sustainable and reach massive scale. The LLC also funds the salaries of the team members for both entities, which provides more flexibility to attract the best talent even though more costly from a tax perspective.

The establishing of the Omidyar Network was based on the conscious decision of the Omidyars to forego substantial amounts of potential tax deductions for their impact investments in order to deploy their capital in initiatives that were outside the focus of traditional philanthropy. The flexible approach has allowed the Omidyar Network to launch and incubate various initiatives that were eventually spun out into separate entities including projects relating to education, financial inclusion, governance, and citizen engagement and "well-being, work and purpose." The Omidyar Network was truly innovative at the time it was launched in 2004, and since then the structure has been adopted by others, most notably the Emerson Collective, the Chan Zuckerberg Initiative and Arnold Ventures, and has attracted the interest of socially conscious family offices, venture capitalists, and institutional investors.[20]

---

[20] The structure is not without critics. For example, Levine questioned the motives of the widow of Apple's Steve Jobs, who created the hybrid Emerson Collective, as being an effort "to transform classic philanthropy by allowing it to operate with the style, culture, and independence that characterize the business from which she derived her wealth". Levine took issue with the lack of public accountability associated with the structure and noted that while the Emerson Collective made traditional philanthropic investments in mentoring and anti-violence programs it also took stakes in publications dedicated to social advocacy and professional sports teams. The hybrid structure certainly provides flexibility for innovation and engaging entrepreneurs in making decisions about supporting new initiatives focused on social change; however, Levine pointed out that

DAFs were first authorized in the early 1990s and have become a valuable strategy for companies wanting to add more formality to their corporate philanthropy beyond direct giving but which are not yet ready to form a new legal entity such as a corporate foundation. Those companies can create a separate fund (although not a separate legal entity) that was held within an existing public charity, such as a local community foundation or the charitable affiliate of a financial services provider. The company contributes funds or assets to the public charity that are allocated to a DAF maintained by the public charity, so named because the company or its designee (e.g., the CEO of the company) retains the right to provide advice or recommendations to the public charity on how grants should be made from the fund and how unused funds should be invested. The DAF is usually named after the company (e.g., "The [name of company] Fund" or "The [name of company] Foundation") and the public charity, as the charitable owner and sponsoring organization of the fund, deducts a small percentage of the fund assets or received contributions as compensation for its services.

DAFs were originally designed to be a relatively simple and inexpensive way for companies to obtain the reputation advantages of a philanthropic foundation and provide companies with the same sort of flexibility from a cash flow and tax deductibility perspective as setting up a corporate foundation as a separate entity (i.e., if the company is having a profitable year it can make a larger tax-deductible contribution to the donor-advised fund, thus reducing the company's current tax bill, and those contributions can be retained in the fund and used in later years to support continuity in the foundation's programs even if the company itself does not have sufficient funds to donate to the DAF in those

Zuckerberg and the Gates Foundation have both failed in well-publicized efforts to fix public education systems and suggested that "greater accountability for public experimentation seems necessary". Levine, M. 2018. "Does the Emerson Collective Square with Philanthropic Accountability?" *Nonprofit Quarterly*, June 11, 2018. For further discussion of hybrid funds, see Mac Cormac, S., J. Finfrock and B. Fox. 2019. "Impact Investing." In *The Lawyer's Corporate Social Responsibility Deskbook*, eds. A. Gutterman et al., 242–243. Chicago: American Bar Association.

years). However, recently they have frequently been used by individuals who have become wealthy as a result of public offerings of shares of the companies that they founded and who decided to create their own DAFs by contributing securities immediately following the offering when the valuations, and resulting tax deduction, were stunningly high. For example, DAFs have been launched by the founders and/or senior executives of Facebook, Netflix, Twitter, Google, WhatsApp, and Microsoft. While these launches often were done with great publicity, the actual impact of these commitments has been questioned by some since DAFs do not have to report on their activities in the same way as corporate foundations. Another criticism is that distributions from DAFs can be deferred indefinitely at the discretion of the donor.[21]

Most asset owners do not have the resources to create structures like the Omidyar Network and will instead rely on intermediaries to identify projects and enterprises that meet the investment and impact goals of the asset owner and execute and manage the investment of the asset owner's capital in those projects and enterprises. The most common form of intermediary structure is a fund, which allows asset owners to pool their resources with other like-minded investors in order to purchase financial instruments issued by social enterprises or other intermediaries. A wide range of impact investment funds are available including mutual funds, exchange-traded funds, money-market funds, venture capital, or private equity funds and hedge funds and asset owners can choose funds based on a number of characteristics such as the types of investment opportunities that the fund managers focus on and the specific environmental and social issues addressed by the companies

---

[21] For further discussion, see Gelles, D. 2018. *A Trendy Philanthropic Loophole.* New York Times, August 5, 2018. B1. See also discussion of "Impact Investing Through Donor-Advised Funds" in Godeke, S., and P. Briaud. 2020. *Impact Investing Handbook: An Implementation Guide for Practitioners*, 107. Rockefeller Philanthropy Advisors. (Exhibit 4–14) (noting the DAFs were the fastest growing philanthropic vehicle as of the end of 2018 and that DAFs provided asset owners with the opportunity to source and recommend investments in private mission-driven businesses, impact funds and nonprofit organizations and to mobilize their assets quickly to create impact).

in the fund's investment portfolio. While funds charge fees for participating, the costs to the asset owner are generally less than if the asset
owner attempted to make the investments directly. Moreover, a well-
selected fund provides the asset owner with access to the experience and
networks of professional managers that understand the impact investment market and are able to assess the risks associated with projects and
enterprises.[22] In addition, funds can forge partnerships with nonprofits
and philanthropic enterprises to create opportunities for fund investors
to purchase investment instruments that are tailored to specific impact
themes such as community development (e.g., support of community-based entrepreneurs) and job training.[23]

The wide range of social impact funds available to asset owners
includes venture capital or private equity funds that operate in accordance with ESG guidelines and seek to make direct investments in enterprises that have a demonstrated focus on achieving direct or indirect
ESG impact through a scalable business model. These funds are typically
organized and structured as for-profit limited partnerships in which the
limited partners are qualified investors that meet specific criteria established under applicable securities laws and the general partner is a group
of impact investing professionals with a strong record of performance in
sourcing, vetting, and selecting impact investments and managing those
investments through engagement with the leadership teams of the fund's

---

[22] Godeke, S. and P. Briaud. 2020. *Impact Investing Handbook: An Implementation Guide for Practitioners*. Rockefeller Philanthropy Advisors, 108. Asset owners may also gain access to professional management expertise without pooling their funds with other investors through the use of "separately managed accounts". See Cautero, R. 2019. "How a Separately Managed Account (SMA) Works." September 11, 2019, https://smartasset.com/investing/separately-managed-account

[23] Id. (describing Benefit Chicago, a collaboration of The Chicago Community Trust, Calvert Impact Capital and the MacArthur Foundation, launched in 2016 to mobilize up to $100 million in impact investments for hard-to-reach commu-
nities and populations in the Chicago region that allowed individuals, corpora-
tions, philanthropies and other investors to purchase from Calvert fixed-income notes that were targeted to Benefit Chicago and collateralized by Calvert's commitment to make the interest payments).

portfolio companies.[24] While limited partners are passive investors in these funds, as required in order for them to limit their exposure for the fund's liabilities to the amount of capital they invested, they do have the right to vote on certain material matters relating to the fund and the general partner is obligated by contract to follow the fund's preexisting investment policies and guidelines. Most funds also have a limited partner advisory committee that includes key investors with relevant experience, such as representatives of organizations involved in activities that are aligned with the environmental and social mission of the fund. Funds often co-invest in portfolio companies with other investment funds or may form a special purpose vehicle with a strategic investor, perhaps one of the limited partners in the fund, to make an investment. In instances where the fund seeks greater involvement in the development and management of an enterprise's business model, the parties may form a joint venture. Finally, the fund's investment guidelines may permit the general partners to use a limited amount of capital to make grants or loans to enterprises; however, the bulk of the fund's holdings will be equity instruments.[25]

---

[24] Limited partnerships, rather than corporations, are used for these types of funds in order to avoid double taxation at the entity and investor levels. While the discussion in this paragraph assumes that the fund is structured as a limited partnership, there is a trend toward structuring funds as LLCs in order to provide all of the participants—investors and the managers of the fund—with the benefits of limited liability (general partners of a limited partnership are potentially subject to unlimited liability, although that risk has been effectively managed by structuring the general partner as an LLC). Like partnerships, LLCs are "pass through" entities for tax purposes, which means that the LLC does not pay taxes on its earnings and such earnings are only taxed at the investor level.

[25] Nonprofits, such as foundations, may invest in social impact funds structured as a partnership or LLC; however, care must be taken to ensure that the underlying investments of the fund do not cause the nonprofit's activities to be characterized by the business of the underlying investment, which puts the nonprofit at risk for unrelated business income tax and a finding that its activities do not exclusively serve the exempt purposes for which it was formed. The typical solution for this potential problem is to form and insert a so-called "blocker corporation" between the nonprofit and fund. Other areas of attention for foundations seeking to engage in investment activities include potential conflicts of interest and issues relating to excess business holdings.

The capital provided by asset owners ultimately ends up under the control of the enterprises that are responsible for carrying out the activities that are intended to create the desired environmental and/or social impact. There are a wide range of possible enterprise structures including public corporations, which are subject to expansive and complex rules regarding disclosures of their activities to shareholders and other members of the investment community, privately held corporations, nonprofit corporations, public charities, LLCs and low-profit LLCs, cooperatives, and benefit corporations.[26] Each structure represents a different way for organizing and managing the inputs that are required in order to carry out an impact-oriented project or initiative. For-profit enterprises seek to create financial value for their owners and collect the capital necessary to fund their operations through the sale of goods and services and the issuance of debt and equity instruments that promise a return of capital to the holders. Nonprofit enterprises also create and distribute goods and services, but do so primarily to contribute to the greater good of society. Impact investors and others that provide capital to nonprofits do so without expectation of financial return.

For-profits and nonprofits can be seen operating side by side in pursuit of common social objectives. For example, nonprofit hospitals are community-oriented institutions driven by mission and purpose rather than shareholder returns, while for-profit hospitals provide the same service but must balance a similar drive for serving communities with providing a satisfactory return on investment to their shareholders. While providing quality health care is the common social and business goal of both nonprofit and for-profit hospitals, nonprofits are able to take a longer-term view of their operations while the managers of for-profit hospitals may be under pressure to generate operational efficiencies and short-term profits that cause them to make decisions that do not align with the needs of the community and health care workers.[27]

---

[26] Godeke, S., and P. Briaud. 2020. *Impact Investing Handbook: An Implementation Guide for Practitioners*, 106 and 108. Rockefeller Philanthropy Advisors, For detailed discussion of social enterprises, see Gutterman, A. Forth Coming. 2021. *Social Enterprises*. Chicago: American Bar Association.

[27] Kahn, K. 2019. "How Do Nonprofit and For-Profit Hospitals Differ? It's Complicated." *Nonprofit Quarterly*, September 10, 2019.

Enterprises are selected based on the application of the various tools available to impact investors including screening and ESG integration and the focus of their business models on themes and environmental/social problems that are of particular concern to the investor such as such as clean energy, green technology, or sustainable agriculture.[28] Enterprises typically prepare their own business plans and make presentations to investors describing the impact goals that management has developed on their own, hopefully in consultation with the individuals and groups who will experience the outcomes from the enterprise's activities. While investors may largely accept the plans developed by the managers of the enterprise, they may also use transactional structures and/or provisions in the contracts governing the investment that are designed to create specific impact outcomes.[29] For example, a debt investment may take the form of a sustainable bond, which is an instrument that requires that the proceeds must be exclusively applied to eligible environmental and/or social projects, such as affordable housing loans targeted at residents who earn less than a community's median income, in order to specifically target positive environmental and/or social impact. Sustainable bonds include Green, Social, and Sustainability Bonds, and one form of Sustainability Bond is a Social Impact Bond based on a "pay-for-success model"

---

[28] In an effort to make the screening process easier for impact investors, B Lab Company ("B Lab"), a Pennsylvania nonprofit corporation which has been a driving force behind the adoption of benefit corporation legislation across the country, has become the certifying body for certification as a Certified B Corp., which offers access to the Certified B Corporation logo often seen as being a "Good Housekeeping Seal of Approval" for sustainable businesses. Certified B corporations and benefit corporations share the same characteristics with respect to accountability and transparency (i.e., directors are required to consider the impact of the company's activities on all stakeholders and a report of overall social and performance assessed against a third party standard must be prepared and publically published), and certified B corporations must also achieve a minimum verified score on a "B Impact Assessment". During the early years of "certified B corporations" there was no requirement that a company also be a benefit corporation in order to be certified; however, from the end of 2017 onward obtaining and maintaining Certified B Corp certification requires benefit corporation status.

[29] Godeke, S., and P. Briaud. 2020. *Impact Investing Handbook: An Implementation Guide for Practitioners (Rockefeller Philanthropy Advisors*, 109.

enabled by public–private partnerships. In a typical situation, a private sector investor provides funds to a local party that will be responsible for implementing a specific social project so as to achieve mutually agreed impact performance targets. At the end of the project, its impacts are measured by an outside outcome evaluator and if the targets are achieved the investors will be paid by the local government as provided under the terms of the bond.[30]

Covenants regarding the operation of the enterprise's business may be included in both debt and equity financings, such as requirements that the funds provided by the investors be deployed in particular locations and/or be used to improve the well-being of specific groups of beneficiaries. In order to demonstrate compliance with the covenants, enterprises will be expected to provide detailed regular reports to investors and submit to independent audits to test the alignment of their performance against the agreed commitments. In addition, as impact investments begin to mature and investors are looking to remove their capital from enterprises that have achieved sustainability, questions have arisen about what steps can and should be taken to ensure that exits are done "responsibly" and that management and the new owners of the enterprise continue to engage in responsible behavior and do not divert from the original mission.[31]

---

[30] For example, BASF SE as a social investor funded a Social Impact Bond ("SIB") to finance a program at the Pestalozzi School in the City of Mannheim that provides additional education support to immigrant children through the City's public school system. Defined outcome goals for the program were defined at the beginning when the SIB was first issued and included an increasing number of recommendations for Gymnasium for children with migrant backgrounds and overall improvement in the cognitive skills for those children. At the end of the program the results will be scientifically evaluated and publicly disclosed and if and only if the pre-defined goals are attained will the City of Mannheim, as the project sponsor and outcomes payor, repay BASF SE's invested capital. Id.

[31] While investors and intermediaries are focused on environmental and/or social impact, they also have to answer to their own investors and fulfill their commitments to those investors to return capital within a specified time frame. For example, the lifecycle of venture capital funds typically runs anywhere from eight to twelve years and near the end of that term the fund managers need to find liquidity for their portfolio investments since many investors in those funds are not interested in, or qualified for, holding the investments directly if

Impact Instruments

The last element of the structure of an impact investment involves the selection of the investment instrument that will be used by the investor or the intermediary to provide capital to the enterprise.[32] The decision depends on a number of factors including the investment goals and risk tolerances of the investor/intermediary; the legal structure of the enterprise; the instruments that the enterprise have previously issued to other investors, since the relative priorities of different groups of investors with respect to return of capital and their rights to the assets of the enterprise as collateral for their investment must always be clear; the relative cost of the financing to the business and the existing owners; the risks associated with the instrument and the degree of flexibility associated with any payment obligations under the terms of the instrument. The discussion below assumes that the enterprise has been formed as a corporation, which means that the equity interests that it can issue will be shares of stock that can have varying rights, preferences, and privileges as provided by statute and negotiations between the parties. Corporations can also issue debt securities and it is possible to provide for the conversion of debt securities into equity securities upon the occurrence of specified events. The default designation for equity securities of enterprises formed as an

---

the fund simply distributes the portfolio to the investors. For further discussion, see Silva, A., and J. Riecke. 2017. "What's "Responsible" about Impact Investing Exits?" Center for Financial Inclusion, March 17, 2017, https://centerforfinancialinclusion.org/whats-responsible-about-impact-investing-exits, and Rozas, D. 2014. *The Art of the Responsible Exit in Microfinance Equity Sales.* Washington DC: Consultative Group to Assist the Poor.

[32] The term "capital" should be understood as including the entire base of tangible and intangible assets of the corporation or, more particularly, that portion of the assets of the corporation, regardless of their source, which will be utilized for the conduct of the corporate business and for the purpose of generating gains and profits which might be available for distribution among the owners of the corporation. This expansive definition of corporate capital includes cash and assets contributed by the ultimate owners of the corporation; cash received from investors in the form of loans; funds generated from the actual operations of the business and from appreciation in the value of the assets used as part of the business; and financing received from non-investment sources (e.g. commercial lenders).

LLC is a "membership interest"; however, LLCs have the flexibility to issue equity securities that are denominated as "shares" and essentially replicate many aspects of the capital structure typically used by corporations. Regardless of which type of instrument is selected, the enterprise must have a clear idea of how the capital will be deployed, the value (both financial and impact) that is anticipated from the use of the funds and the methods that will be available to investors to recover their investment within a time frame that is aligned with their specific investment goals.

Equity securities, including common shares and preferred shares, are the foundation of the corporate capital structure. Equity securities evidence the holders' rights with respect to the long-term earnings and asset appreciation. Accordingly, particularly in the case of common shareholders, such stakeholders may be more willing to reinvest current profits in worthwhile investment projects that will ultimately increase the value of the corporation. In contrast to debt securities discussed below, the capital contributed by holders of equity securities typically is permanent, and the corporation is not obligated to return to the shareholders any amounts that they have invested in the business. In other words, there is generally no assurance that common and preferred shareholders will not suffer the loss of their entire investment while other claimants (i.e., debtholders) recover all or a portion of the capital that they provided to the corporation. As among themselves, preferred shareholders have priority over common shareholders in terms of repayment and the terms of preferred stock often provide for interim payments to preferred shareholders, in the form of dividends, which may be tied to achievement of certain performance milestones agreed upon at the time that the shares are issued. Common shareholders have what is often referred to as a "residual interest" in the assets of the corporation and their rights to repayment are not only subordinated to all forms of preferred stock but also to all government claims or taxes, employee claims recognized by law (e.g., pension obligations) and all bank and trade debt.

A return on investment for equity investors depends on the successful performance of the enterprise and its ability to create an exit path for the investors (e.g., a public offering or a sale of the enterprise to an outside party). So-called straight preferred stock, which carries a fixed date for redemption of the shares and return of principal to the shareholder, is a limited exception to the rule that equity securities are permanent capital. The asset classes associated with equity securities are "public equity," which includes investing in the widely held and liquid common shares of so-called public companies and "private equity," which includes the common practice of venture capital funds providing funding to innovative impact-focused startups through the purchase of preferred stock. Although at common law, and in the absence of any statute or agreement to the contrary, all equity securities enjoyed equal rights and privileges, it is now the prevailing practice to divide equity securities into two or more classes with varying rights, preferences, and privileges as to the payment of dividends, liquidating distributions, redemption, conversion, and voting rights.

Debt securities are obligations of the corporation and are treated as part of its liabilities. There are an unlimited number of types of debt instruments, ranging from a simple non-negotiable promissory note containing little more than the corporation's promise to pay to a capital note or other long-form instrument, which contains elaborate provisions with respect to defaults, remedies, security, covenants, and, in some cases, voting rights similar to those granted to shareholders. When referring to debt securities, the principal amount owed is the "principal"; the date when repayment of the principal is due is termed the "maturity date"; and the rate of interest being paid is often called the "coupon rate." Debt securities may be either long or short term, pre-payable (or callable), convertible into another security, subordinated to certain classes of other creditors, and may even provide for participation in the earnings of the company (e.g., payments over the term of the instrument may be linked to the amount of profits generated by the company, perhaps in addition to fixed payments that must be made regardless of performance). As a general rule, debt securities are issued in denominations of $1,000 or multiples thereof, and are quoted based on a percentage of the principal amount.

A versatile "hybrid" form of financing instrument is an equity or debt instrument that allows an investor to change, or "convert," the original security into a different class of equity securities or into another form of corporate obligation. These instruments are referred to as convertible securities. For example, it may be possible to issue convertible preferred shares that provide an investor with a guaranteed return of dividends for as long as the preferred shares are outstanding, as well as the right to convert the preferred shares into common shares in the future in order to share in any appreciation in the value of the underlying business. A convertible security is really just an outstanding equity or debt security that has been supplemented by a right, upon the occurrence of specified events to "convert" the original security, without payment of additional consideration, into another type of security of the issuer which has been specified in the terms of the original security. For example, a convertible equity security may be preferred shares that can be converted into common shares of the issuer. Some corporate debt instruments may include the right to convert the outstanding principal and interest into common shares of the issuer.[33] Whenever senior securities are convertible into junior securities, it is referred to as downstream conversion. However, it is also possible to provide that junior securities can be converted into a more senior securities in what is referred to as an upstream conversion, although the conversion usually must not impair the rights of the existing creditors of the corporation.

Some investment structures involve the issuance of warrants, which evidence a right granted by the corporation to the holder to purchase shares of stock or debt securities at certain times and prices. The exercise price for a warrant, sometimes referred to as the "strike price," is often higher than the current value of the underlying securities. While warrants can be issued independently, they are commonly issued in companion with nonconvertible equity or debt securities in order to provide prospective investors with an extra item of value that might convince them to purchase the principal security. However, the issuance of warrants may not have the desired effect in inducing the investor to provide

---

[33] A popular form of financing for startups is the issuance of convertible notes before the company has secured equity financing, with such notes providing that they will be converted into the equity instrument, typically Series A Preferred Stock, issued by the company in its first round of outside financing from professional investors such as venture capitalists. Purchasers of the convertible notes are "rewarded" for taking on the risk of an early stage investment through a discount on the conversion price in relation to the price being paid by the outside investors for their Series A Preferred shares.

funds to the corporation since, in a sense, the corporation's issuance of warrants is a "bet" that it will not be as successful as the investor purchasing the warrants expects it will be. If management were more optimistic about the enterprise's prospects, it would not issue warrants, but rather would wait and sell common stock after the price has risen and rely on alternative sources of financing, such as commercial loans or short-term debt securities, in the interim. Corporations that issue warrants are not guaranteed access to the additional funds that would be received if the warrants are exercised and the investor's decision about whether or not to exercise a warrant will depend on the performance of the enterprise and other investment opportunities available to the investor at the time that the decision is being made. Warrants may be issued in conjunction with a debt instrument with the assumption, but not the requirement, that the warrants will eventually be exercised by converting the then-outstanding principal and interest owed on the debt instrument.

Distribution and Liquidation Priorities

While the capital received from various sources is rarely segregated, and cash is essentially a fungible resource, there are clear demarcations as to the legal claims that capital providers will have with respect to the assets of the corporation upon the cessation of its business operations. The relative priorities among the various financial stakeholders in the corporation are important to understand most of the legal and business aspects of corporate financing and can be illustrated by reference to the order in which a corporation's assets would be distributed upon liquidation in bankruptcy proceedings.

The secured creditors include all parties that have advanced funds to the corporation and received a mortgage (i.e., security interest) on specific corporate assets, as well as certain other parties who may have liens on the corporation's assets as a matter of law (e.g., a landlord's lien for nonpayment of rent; an artisan's lien to secure payment for services supplied in connection with a chattel (e.g., an automobile repair); and a warehouseman's lien to secure the nonpayment of storage charges) or otherwise (e.g., a creditor's efforts to satisfy an outstanding obligation by going to court may result in a judicial lien). Investors in this group include secured debtholders who enjoy a senior position among corporate investors. Their anticipated return on investment is generally limited to the amount invested plus interest thereon; however, they enjoy a first claim against the assets pledged as security for fulfillment of the company's obligations. As such, they trade at a lower rate of return, relative to more junior securities, for the highest level of safety. If the claims of a particular secured creditor exceed the value of their security interest (e.g., the asset subject to the mortgage or other lien) the excess amount will be treated in the same way as a claim of an unsecured creditor. Priority creditors have the first preference to the proceeds of the sale of those assets that are not subject to mortgages or other such liens. Priority creditors include the Internal Revenue Service, people with certain kinds of wage claims, and people who have supplied services to the company in administering any formal insolvency proceedings (i.e., bankruptcy).

Any cash or other assets left after satisfaction of the secured creditors and priority claims goes to the remaining (i.e., unsecured) creditors of the corporation, pro rata according to the amount owed to each. This class often includes investors who purchase unsecured debt securities of the corporation. Like secured debtholders, the investment return of unsecured debtholders is limited to the amount invested plus interest thereon; however, the obligations of the corporation are not backed by a pledge of assets. Accordingly, unsecured debtholders are within the lower priority class of unsecured creditors, and their claims are junior to those of secured debtholders. This enhanced level of "risk" generally leads to a higher interest rate on unsecured debt than on secured debt. This type of unsecured debt is often referred to as "mezzanine finance" and includes subordinated loans, participating loans, and instruments that combine elements of debt and equity such as convertible bonds and bonds with warrants. Non-investor unsecured creditors of the corporation will include trade creditors (i.e., those persons who have previous supplied goods and services to the corporation).

After satisfaction of all the claims of the various creditors, the remaining cash and assets of the corporation will be distributed among the equity claimants; first to the preferred shareholders, and then the remainder to the residual owners of the company, the common shareholders.

CHAPTER 4

Organizing for Impact Investment

In this chapter we consider various issues and actions to be taken in relation to designing and implementing an organizational framework for engaging in impact investing. As we have seen, there is a wide range of impact investors and each of them has their own unique set of investment and impact goals. In addition, institutions and other organizational forms which assume responsibility for investing the assets of others, such as foundations, endowments, and investment funds, have legal responsibilities as fiduciaries of the ultimate owners of the assets that are being invested. Each asset owner must address the fundamental questions raised in this chapter and establish a sufficient level of internal formality to build the team and other resources necessary to make good decisions about impact investing, even if those decisions are limited to the selection of intermediaries to actively manage the assets on a day-to-day basis. Intermediaries, such as fund managers, must also create an organizational framework for impact investing that can be explained to their prospective investors. This process will be illustrated later in the chapter when we discuss formation of impact investment funds. The opening sections generally assume that the organizational process is being carried out by a foundation.

Organizing should begin with visiting (or revisiting) a series of fundamental questions and issues relating to the investment and impact motivations and goals of the asset owner or fund manager.[1] Simply put, this is

---

[1] When used herein, the term "fund manager" should be construed broadly to include managers of the full range of intermediaries described in the previous chapter including charities and other nonprofit organizations that pool contributions from a number of investors and impact investment funds including mutual funds, exchange-traded funds, money-market funds, venture capital, or private equity funds and hedge funds.

the time to wrestle with the fundamental question of what is the owner or manager is looking to achieve by engaging in impact investing. A simple, yet comprehensive, framework for preparing to launch an impact investing programs recommended by Rockefeller Philanthropy Advisors (RPA) involves consideration of the following[2]:

- *Why is the asset owner/manager interested in impact investing?* Asset owners and fund managers may have several reasons for considering impact investing including a desire to have a social impact, an interest in integrating traditional investment focused on financial return with philanthropic activities, an interest in supporting the development of innovative technologies by social entrepreneurs looking to implement those technologies to address social problems, a belief that market forces can contribute to the pursuit of social good, an interest in using data and sophisticated data analysis to optimize potential impact, a belief that capital markets can expand the scope of impact beyond traditional philanthropic initiatives, and a recognition that impact investing can provide competitive financial returns.
- *What type of changes is the asset owner/manager seeking to achieve through impact investing?* Many investors begin with a list of broad categories such as poverty, health, climate change, and/or education, or look for opportunities to invest in funds, enterprises and projects that are focused on specific challenges (e.g., delivery of innovative educational technology), populations (e.g., women, children, elderly, people of color, or people with disabilities), locations (e.g., a specific neighborhood area) or institutions (e.g., advocacy organizations, hospitals, schools or charities). Another approach is to provide support for various parts of an ecosystem created for the development and deployment of innovative technologies to address a range of social problems.

---

[2] Impact Investing: Strategy and Action (Rockefeller Philanthropy Advisors Philanthropy Roadmap), 3–10.

- *How does the asset owner/manager intend to assess progress toward achievement of the goals for impact investment and the desired changes from impact investing?* Asset owners and fund managers must select appropriate tools for measuring the social impact of their investments alongside financial returns and have metrics and processes for measurement in place before each investment is made. When setting financial and impact targets, consideration must be given to the risks associated with achieving those targets. Financial risk is an intensely studied and well understood concept; however, the art and science of impact risk is still emerging and metrics are imprecise. For example, using impact investing to support the development of innovative technology not only involves risks that the development efforts will fail and/or the technology will not lead to the anticipated social outcomes, but also may lead to unintended consequences and negative effects.

- *When does the asset owner/manager expect to realize the antic-ipated financial and impact returns on the impact investment?* The scope of the challenges that are typically addressed by impact investing generally requires more patience on the part of investors than traditional investments. When the goal is to develop and implement innovative technologies to address a given social problem, the process may take several years and the efforts will likely run into unanticipated problems that will slow progress. While the end result will hopefully be sub-stantial social impact and a strong financial return, it will take time and impact investors need to be comfortable with longer time horizons for both social change and financial return.

- *Who does the asset owner/manager need to work with in order to achieve success and growth?* While an asset owner or fund manager can have social impact acting alone, sustainable success and growth comes from working with others and asset owners and fund managers must decide on who they will look to for help in identifying and management impact investment opportunities. Asset owners and fund managers generally seek to put together a group of investment and professional (i.e., legal, tax, and accounting) advisors and build connections with peers in the investment and philanthropic communities who can share experiences and best practices (and offer chances to learn through co-investment, which is also a good way to allocate additional capital to worth projects in order to accelerate and broaden their impact). Asset owners and fund managers must also consider their appetite and resources for engaging with management of enterprises in which direct investments are made and, in the case of asset owners, the fund managers that they select as their intermediaries.

The answers to each of these questions are the inputs that the asset owner or fund manager needs to effectively prepare for engaging in impact investing and the answers should provide the asset owner or fund manager with a good idea of the level of readiness for actually getting started and the information that is necessary in order to prepare certain investment governance documents that can be used as guides for organizing impact investing activities and creating and implementing the investment strategy. The asset owner or fund manager should also establish a plan for achieving "investor readiness," which RPA has described as requiring clearly defined implementation goals and strategies, including a relevant timeline; consensus with key stakeholders, such as family, board, staff, and others; relevant experience and expertise, internally from staff or externally from advisors; organizational momentum and capacity, such as processes and systems; and an intentional approach to building the portfolio and finding and managing impact investment opportunities.[3]

Investment Governance Documents

RPA recommends that impact investors formalize their theory of change and investment and impact goals by developing and implementing an impact investment statement (IIS) and an investment policy statement (IPS). RPA described the IIS is a guiding tool for both internal

---

[3] Godeke, S., and P. Briaud. 2020. *Impact Investing Handbook: An Implementation Guide for Practitioners*, 147. Rockefeller Philanthropy Advisors.

and external stakeholders, which provides clarity of mission, principles, and impact strategy and which generally includes all or most of the following elements: mission, vision, and values; views on fiduciary duty; definition and boundaries of impact investing; role of impact investing; impact investing approaches; theory of change; impact goals; impact tools and structures; product examples; and approach to impact evaluation. Suggested topics for the IPS include the roles and responsibilities of the board, the investment committee, and the ultimate asset owners; role of advisors, including level of discretion; overall investment goals and objectives; risk appetite; liquidity requirements; diversification goals; investment limitations, including specific assets and transactions; tax considerations, as applicable; asset allocation strategy; time horizon; new cash investment guidelines; and financial reporting. Investors may create two separate statements or integrate everything into a single document; however, the important point is that the investor establishes the guiding principles normally associated with an IIS to provide a point of reference for execution of the investment and impact strategy (i.e., design of investment products and portfolios) in line with the IPS topics.[4]

Implementation Goals and Building Consensus

Preparation of the IIS and IPS should be among the first implementation goals for any asset owner or fund manager; however, there are always going to be additional activities that need to be addressed early in the process in order to be sure that the entire program can be rolled out smoothly. Implementation goals will depend on the prior experiences of the asset owner or fund manager with impact investing, if any, available resources and the concerns of the key parties involved in making investing decisions. In order to know how to proceed, the asset owner or fund manager should analyze its existing investment portfolio and practices and survey the practices and activities of its peers. Among other things, this informs the asset owner or fund manager of the methods that have been used in the past to evaluate potential investment opportunities and

---

[4] Adapted from Godeke, S., and P. Briaud. 2020. *Impact Investing Handbook: An Implementation Guide for Practitioners*, 88–90. Rockefeller Philanthropy Advisors.

often uncovers current investments that might not be consistent with the asset owner's overall investment and impact objectives. An easy way to get comfortable with using the tools of impact investing is to apply them to an existing portfolio, such as by using screening methods or evaluating the investments using ESG integration methodologies.

Another important goal should be educating all of the relevant decision makers (e.g., board and investment committee members, family members and/or staff members) on the tools of impact investing and the potential benefits from implementing an impact investing strategy. In situations where there is a high level of skepticism, care should be taken to clearly demonstrate how impact investment tools can be used (e.g., applying basic screening tools to investment opportunities in a sector or thematic area that is already familiar to the organization) and select initial investments that have a higher probability of success with a reasonable level of risk and which are accompanied by investment and impact metrics that are easy to understand (e.g., a loan to a nonprofit that has already been vetted by the organization that can be tied to supporting a particular impact project that is readily understood by organizational leaders). The objective is to build a consensus among all of the organizational stakeholders that impact investing makes sense and is a path that should be pursued. This is not necessarily an easy task, since it often involves fundamental changes in organizational culture and requires that persons and groups learn new tools and concepts and set aside long-held views on investment objectives and the roles of various institutions in driving societal changes. In addition to creating the IIS and IPS, fundamental changes may be required in the organization's overall mission statement and strategic plans.

RPA provided several strategies for approaching and engaging with various persons and groups within the organization in order to build a consensus around impact investing including helping them understand why the organization is embarking on a path of impact investing using approaches and language tailored to the specific audience; demonstrating how impact investing has an appropriate place among all the tools that should be deployed to achieve the organization's mission; leveraging advocates, partners, stories, and data to support the case for impact investing; focusing on integrating and aligning financial and impact goals in the investment process; and selecting a diverse group of representatives from among all the stakeholders to assume a more formal role in impact investment decision making and oversight.[5]

The entire process takes time—organizations should generally expect that establishing an implementation plan that has support from throughout the organization will take anywhere from six to twelve months—and should be viewed as a continuous activity that will extend well into the future and include ongoing engagement with internal and external stakeholders, updating information and data regarding impact investing and education on new and emerging impact investing tools. During the initial implementation period, the organization can start slowly with modest impact investment activities such as a small program-related investment (PRI) that allows all the members of the team to gain experience in identifying and conducting due diligence on investment opportunities and establishing procedures for monitoring performance. Co-investing with private or corporate foundations pursuing a similar mission is also a good way to get started and demonstrate the potential of impact investing to the board of directors and members of the investment team.

Identifying and Selecting Investment Advisors

Many impact investors rely on one or more investment advisors to serve as intermediaries in the impact investing process. The number of advisors, and their respective roles, will depend on several factors, notably the skills and experiences of the impact investor's internal team, which is discussed in more detail below, and the investor's need to have advisors that can contribute to identifying and vetting impact investment opportunities. Investment advisors generally focus their activities on investment management and may or may not have "discretion" to actually make decisions about which impact investments should be purchased and/or sold on behalf of the investor. In addition, impact advisors may provide other services in areas such legal, tax and accounting.

While advisors can and should be able to help impact investors with setting their goals with respect to financial return and impact, investors

---

[5] Id. at 149.

should have a clear understanding of their goals before searching for an advisor. In addition, impact investors should develop a list of the services that they would expect to need from an advisor. Focusing on goals and services allows the impact investor to set their own unique set of selection criteria and narrow the search for potential candidates. While impact investors may seek recommendations from peers about investment advisors, the preferred approach is to do an open solicitation that reaches a broad range of advisors and provides the investor with an opportunity to identify important selection factors such as a specific thematic background and experience in advising on investments in certain types of projects or locations. Impact investors should also seek advisors with a track record of working successfully with clients that are similar in size and experience to the investor. The selection process generally includes preliminary screening followed by in-person interviews and review of formal proposals from a small group of finalists. RPA suggested that impact investors adhere to the following guiding principles when selecting their advisors[6]:

- Do they have expertise at the intersection of your impact and investment goals? And do they have specific examples of their experience and the role they played in desired strategies and investments?
- Do they have credentials to satisfy the work requirement and satisfy your key stakeholders?
- Do they have experience working with organizations and governance structures like yours? For example, do they operate on a discretionary or nondiscretionary basis?
- Can they speak your language and help you reach your specific goals? Do they exhibit values alignment with you on how they operate as an organization?
- Are they able to measure impact in line with your goals?
- What are their business strengths and weaknesses: customer service, reporting capabilities, ability and willingness to customize, fees, etc.?

---

[6] Id. at 152.

As mentioned above, investment advisors should bring skills, experience, and contacts to the impact investor's process that may not yet be available internally and the investor should expect that the advisor will assist in building internal capacity. However, impact investors should not rely completely on their advisors and should look for support from organizations of their peers that provide events, education, training, data, and information on "best practices" that investors can readily access and apply to their own situations. The goal of all this should be capacity building to support an organizational transition from traditional financial-focused investment and/or philanthropy at the two ends of a broad spectrum toward impact investing, which combines financing and social impact returns. Among other things, steps should be taken to build capacities in understanding the fiduciary duties associated with impact investing (as discussed below); impact principles, frameworks, and standards; relevant public policies and regulations, such as Opportunity Zones; forms of social enterprises, such as benefit corporations; and impact measurement and reporting.[7]

Building the Impact Investment Team

Impact investors, whether they are the actual asset owners or fund managers overseeing the assets of others, need to build and maintain an internal team with the requisite skills and experience for effective and successful impact investing. Some investors may already have teams in place that have been handling traditional financial investment and philanthropic activities as separate functions. In those situations, the challenge is to merge the functions without getting bogged down in conflicts based on different cultures and a lack of understanding between the two groups

---

[7] RFA suggested a number of peer organizations focusing on aspects of venture philanthropy and impact investment including the Asian Venture Philanthropy Network, Confluence Philanthropy, Catalytic Capital Consortium, the Case Foundation, European Venture Philanthropy Association, Global Impact Investing Network, Global Steering Group for Impact Investing, The ImPact, Mission Investor Exchange, Principles for Responsible Investment, Skoll World Forum, Social Capital Markets, and Toniic. Id. at 152 and 173.

as to how they work and the tools that they are used to using. Different processes and systems will be needed and the two groups will need to settle on the best way to communicate and interact. RPA noted that the following questions should be asked as the integration process plays out[8]:

- How deeply does each party need/want to engage?
- If there is more than one team or person, how is the due diligence process being shared?
- What is the right frequency of meetings between investment-oriented and impact-oriented team members?
- How can more intentional communication be encouraged between investment and impact personnel?
- How do roles change from strategy through individual investment selection?
- How do roles change throughout the investment process from sourcing to due diligence, selection, monitoring, and exit?

Integration should work as time goes by and new hires chosen specifically for their specific credentials relating to impact investing join the mix and providing training to everyone working on the team.

The necessary expertise for impact investing can be placed into various roles (e.g., staff, advisors and consultants, or investment committee members) and the skills that will be required will depend on the impact investor's own goals and interests. For example, impact investors should recruit personnel with experience deploying the specific impact investing tools that have been selected and the investor's preferred asset classes, such as screening the ESG performance of publicly traded equities. In situations where the impact investor is unable to find someone to fill a particular role, a consultant or advisor can be brought in to cover that area until a good candidate for a permanent position can be identified. Regardless of the decisions made on internal staffing and the use of advisors and consultants, impact investors that contemplate making a wide range of investments over an extended period of time should serious consider forming an external investment advisory committee that includes experts in the impact investing process that also share a commitment to

---

[8] Id. at 156.

the investor's specific mission and provide experience in identifying and vetting investment opportunities that are consistent with the investor's IIS and IPS. The roles and responsibilities of investment advisory committee members should be carefully developed and clearly stated and may include prospecting for potential investment opportunities, providing training and technical support to internal staff members, reviewing proposed investments against the criterion laid out in the IIS and IPS and, where practical and appropriate, engaging with the managers of the funds or enterprises chosen to receive capital from the impact investor. The investment advisory committee is *not* the investment committee established by the IPS, instead its role is to advise and support the investment committee and the investor's internal team and be available as a resource to other interested parties such as board members.[9]

While the organizational framework for impact investing needs to be designed and built to carry out a range of different functions, the most important output will obviously be the decisions that are made regarding the how the available funds will be invested. The RPA noted that the IPS should include clear guidelines on investment decision making and answer the following questions: who has the responsibility to vote on/approve issues, such as asset allocation or hiring an asset manager; who provides advice or formal recommendations; who reviews and provides oversight on the decision; who implements the decision and who is notified as an interested party?[10] The RPA also suggested the following structure and instruments formalizing the relationships among board members, the investment committee and outside investment advisors in a situation in which discretion regarding investment decisions has been given to the advisor(s)[11]:

- *Board of Directors:* Responsible for developing and approving the IIS and IPS, with the IPS serving as the codification of the

---

[9] The investment committee may also form an *internal* advisory committee to provide support in sourcing investment opportunities, conducting due diligence and creating the processes and systems discussed below.

[10] Godeke, S., and P. Briaud. 2020. *Impact Investing Handbook: An Implementation Guide for Practitioners*, 157. Rockefeller Philanthropy Advisors.

[11] Id. at 159.

relationship between the board and the investment committee; setting the spending and payout policy including the
allocation of the overall investment portfolio to impact investing and targets for financial return and impact outcomes; and
establishing and managing the code of ethics

- *Investment Committee:* Responsible for the duties and activities described in the IPS including selection and management
of external investment advisors pursuant to an investment/
advisory services agreement; reviewing asset allocation; establishing rebalancing policies and ranges; organizing internal
and external advisory committees; and regularly reporting to
the board on portfolio performance

- *External Investment Advisor(s):* Reporting to the investment
committee, external investment advisors are responsible for
carry out their responsibilities under the investment/advisory
services agreement including reviewing and recommending
asset allocation, conducting fund manager due diligence,
selecting, and monitoring investments, reporting on investment performance, rebalancing within asset allocation ranges,
and monitoring IPS compliance

Processes and Systems

Implementing and executing an impact investment program requires
that several important processes and systems be put in place, either by
designing something completely new or making changes to existing practices. Among the areas that need to be considered by foundations moving
toward impact investing are the following[12]:

- *Governance:* Processes for board and investment committee
review and sign off on investments and tracking performance
and reporting

---

[12] Id. at 158 (also recommending use of various tools such as grants or portfolio
management software, customer-relationship management systems, project management systems and document management systems).

- *Legal:* Professional review of any new impact investments and related documentation, particularly relevant for direct investing
- *Administration:* Grants personnel executing expenditure responsibility for any charitable investment, including relevant reporting
- *Accounting:* Finance teams tracking repayments and accounting for impact investments on financial statements and tax returns (e.g., Form 990-PF)
- *Reporting:* Developing and tracking combined impact and financial metrics and creating a process for reporting to key internal and external stakeholders

Legal Considerations

Persons and entities undertaking to manage the investment assets of another, either by making investment directly or providing advice for which the advisor is compensated, must conform to applicable legal and regulatory requirements, some of which are established by statute and others have been developed over long periods through judicial decisions and administrative rulings. Most importantly, managers and advisors must satisfy certain fiduciary duties to the asset owners, notably the prudent investment rules that require fiduciaries to invest and manage property held in a trust as a prudent investor would, by considering the purposes, terms and other circumstances of the trust and by pursuing an overall investment strategy reasonably suited to the trust. The fiduciary duties of asset managers and advisors are often broken down into two types of basic responsibilities[13]:

- *Duty of Care:* The duty of care includes, among other things, the duty to provide advice that is in the best interest of the client (i.e., the asset owner), the duty to seek best execution of a client's transactions where the adviser is responsible for

---

[13] *SEC Adopts Interpretive Guidance on Investment Adviser Fiduciary Duty.* Shearman & Sterling. June 27, 2019.

selecting broker-dealers to execute client trades, and the duty to provide advice and monitoring throughout the relationship. In general, the duty of care requires a manager or advisor to make a reasonable inquiry into its clients' objectives and to have a reasonable belief that the advice it provides is in the best interest of the client based on those objectives.

- *Duty of Loyalty:* The duty of loyalty requires that managers and advisers not subordinate their clients' interests to their own, which means that managers and advisers must make full and fair disclosure to their clients of all material facts relating to the management or advisory relationship, including the capacity in which the manager or adviser is acting with respect to the services provided, and eliminate or expose through disclosure all conflicts of interest that might incline the manager or advisor to render advice or take other actions that are not disinterested.

In addition, managers and advisers, as well as directors, trustees, and members of the investment committee, are subject to several ancillary fiduciary duties that apply to foundations and endowments under state statutes that are based on model laws such as the Uniform Prudent Management of Institutional Funds Act (UPMIFA), which applies generally to all entities, and the Uniform Prudent Investor Act, which applies specifically to trusts, including a duty to investigate (i.e., make a reasonable effort to verify facts relevant to fund management and investment), a duty of obedience (i.e., perform duties with loyalty to the entity's mission and obedience to nonprofit purposes), and duty to minimize costs by only incurring reasonable costs in the course of managing the assets.

Historically, the duties of care and loyalty have been applied almost exclusively in the context of traditional investment activities, which means financial prudence has generally been the paramount factor in any specific investment decision. However, foundations, endowments, and other nonprofits must be mindful of the duty of obedience in making investment decisions, with one court explaining that this duty "requires the director of a not-for-profit corporation to be faithful to the purposes and goals of the organization, since unlike business corporations, whose ultimate objective is to make money, nonprofit corporations are defined by their specific objectives."[14] In fact, the UPMIFA allows for mission considerations to be taken into account and for allocating assets to programs that have a mission purpose. In addition, the UPMIFA permits consideration of an asset's special relationship or special value, if any, to the charitable purposes of the institution as part of any analysis of the prudence of a particular investment. RPA notes that fiduciary duties across the entire portfolio of a foundation or endowment can be satisfied through a combination of financial and impact prudence, which means that a portfolio can include a balanced allocation of assets (e.g., traditional financial investments from the endowment to preserve and grow principal) and distributions (e.g., PRIs at below market rate that meet charitable standards and/or grants that meet charitable standards, all of which are allowed under principles of impact prudence).[15]

Clearly fiduciary duties are fundamental concerns for all types of investors, especially foundations and other nonprofits, and it is important to create a formal framework within the overall impact investing process to avoid and/or manage conflicts of interest, both actual and perceived, and analyze compliance with the complex rules that apply to PRIs. Problems in this area can tarnish the investor's image and lead to legal and regulatory issues with the IRS and states' attorney general offices, which are typically charged with overseeing the activities of charitable organizations. It is important to create, approve, and enforce a robust conflicts of interest policy and to carefully document compliance with the policy with respect to each of the investments in the portfolio.

---

[14] Manhattan Eye, Ear and Throat Hospital v. Spitzer, 186 Misc. 2d 126, at 152 (NY, 1999).

[15] Godeke, S., and P. Briaud. 2020. *Impact Investing Handbook: An Implementation Guide for Practitioners* (Rockefeller Philanthropy Advisors, 2020), 164. For discussion of other legal consideration, such expenditure responsibilities, self-dealing, excess benefit transactions and tax and accounting consideration for PRIs, see Id. at 165–167.

Building an Implementation Plan

Establishing goals, building a team of internal talent and external advisors, and understanding the relevant legal considerations are all important steps in creating the implementation plan for the impact investing program. The plan needs to be comprehensive on touch in each of the usual stages for a particular investment beginning with determining whether an opportunity fits within the investor's financial and impact goals and then continue through due diligence, executing the investment, monitoring the performance of the investment, and, eventually, exiting the investment. Each of these stages will require a specific set of participants being their experiences and tools to the process. According to RPA and others, the key components of an implementation plan generally include clear goals and scope; a description of the overall roles for internal and external resources; a timeline with milestones or deliverables; budgets and schedules of other resources required for implementation of the plan; description of risks, assumptions, and contingencies relating to the goals and the execution of the plan itself; strategies for communications with stakeholders (including external communications on the investor's website and in public presentations) and managing stakeholder expectations; a plan for effecting required changes in organizational culture to embed impact investing and its associated goals and mission; and a framework for documenting the entire investment process and preserving related records such as internal memorandums and minutes of the deliberations of the board of directors and investment committee.[16]

Formation and Management of Impact Investment Funds

The discussion above illustrates the process that foundations, endowments, and family offices might follow in organizing the activities necessary to pursue an impact investing strategy. One of the many choices that those asset owners must make is whether to place all or a portion of their assets in the hands of intermediaries including investment funds

---

[16] Id. at 167, 169 and 173.

promoted and operated by managers promising experience and skills in identifying and managing impact investment opportunities. Investment fund managers need to address all of the same questions and issues confronting their prospective investors—what is their "theory of change," what tools will they use to screen and select investments, do they have the right team members and what policies and procedures should be put in place to manage deal flow and measure performance—and must be prepared to demonstrate to those investors why they are an appropriate vehicle for them to realize their investment and impact goals.

There are many different categories of impact investment funds: hedge and mutual funds, which generally look to achieve market or premium returns on their investments with positive social or environmental impact as a secondary goal and follow either responsible impact investing (negative screening to identify and eliminate environmental, social, and governance (ESG) risks) or sustainable impact investing (positive screening to identify ESG opportunities) strategies, or private equity and venture capital funds, which usually focus on strategies based on thematic (targeting specific types of environmental or social issues) or "impact first" (prioritizing impact over financial returns) investing.[17] Funds are available to appeal to the wide range of preferences among impact investors regarding the stage of development of their portfolio companies, the type of investment instrument, the size of their investment, the timing of their return on investment, and the manner in which they expect to exit the investment opportunity. For example, some investors prefer funds that focus on providing seed capital to assist startups in the initial stages of building the business, even before the time that the company seeks to raise larger amounts of capital in its first full venture capital financing. Other investors will have a somewhat lower tolerance for risk and will usually only be willing to participate in funds that make later-stage investments in companies that have already proven the viability of their business models and offer more favorable exit opportunities within a short- or medium-term investment horizon.

---

[17] https://impact.mofo.com/funding-financing/social-impact-funds-structuring-considerations/

Private equity and venture capital funds focused on impact investing are typically organized as a limited partnership or a limited liability company (LLC). The investors in these funds are institutional investors, foundations, charities, endowments, and wealthy individuals who have contributed cash to the limited partnership or LLC for investment and management by managers with experience in working with small, emerging "high-risk" ventures with a business model that promises both traditional financial return and significant positive environmental and/or social impact.[18] The diversity of the investor base for impact investment funds has expanded in recent years and most of the investors have incorporate environmental and social impact into their own formal set of internal investment guidelines. The funds are invested in 15–25 "portfolio companies," assuming a fund size of about $200 million (the average size of an impact investment fund as of 2016), and the managers will typically review thousands of business plans. Funds may supply all of the capital required by a portfolio company for a specific round of investment or the fund managers may participate in co-investments into portfolio companies with other funds and/or strategic investors (using a special purpose vehicle) or form a joint venture with a portfolio company directly. If permitted under the terms of fund's investment policies, the fund managers may also make direct loans or grants to portfolio companies, although equity investments are the primary focus.[19]

---

[18] Participation of certain types of investors in an impact investment fund may lead to complex additions to the basic structure, although experienced fund managers should be able to make the necessary accommodations fairly easily and flexibility to make the changes will be built into the partnership or operating agreement from the beginning. For example, nonprofits will be concerned that by investing in fund structures as a "pass-through entity" for tax purposes (i.e., a partnership or LLC) the underlying investments of a fund will cause their activities to be characterized by the business of the underlying investment, thereby raising the risks of unrelated business income tax and that their activities do not exclusively serve its exempt purposes. These issues will typically be addressed by inserting a corporate blocker in between the nonprofit entity and the underlying partnership or LLC. Id.

[19] Id.

The funds are long-term businesses with a life expectancy of 10–12 years, and most of the investments are made during the first several years of the fund's duration with the expectation that they will mature into an exit opportunity before the end of the term of fund.[20] While the managers only contribute a nominal amount (e.g., 1 percent) to the funds, they receive a disproportionate allocation of the profits. For example, it is common for profits to be allocated 20 percent to the managers and 80 percent to the investors, thereby providing tremendous incentives to the managers to maximize the return from an investment in a company (profits also received preferred tax treatment as capital gains). Managers will also receive some form of management fee to cover salaries and other overhead expenses over the term of the fund. Assuming they are successful with their initial fund, the managers will usually operate more than one fund at a time.[21]

Limited partnerships and LLCs are used for impact investing funds to provide investors with certain tax benefits including avoidance of double taxation if the corporate form was used and to provide investors with limited liability with respect to the operations of the fund: the liability of the investors will be limited to the total amount of cash that they contribute to the fund. In exchange for limited liability, investors must surrender

---

[20] While liquidation is generally done by selling securities in the fund's portfolio and distributing the cash to fund investors there are instances where the securities themselves are distributed to the investors, although most investors prefer that the fund managers make the decisions regarding holding or disposing investments since they are in a better position to understand how the underlying businesses are operated.

[21] A number of databases have been created to collect and present information on impact investment opportunities, both funds and products. For example, RPA has prepared a library of impact investment profiles that include a table with a snapshot of the proposed impact and investment, an overview of the impact to identify the problem/need, a description of the market and the investment's proposed response. Investors can learn about the fund's impact approach, themes, sectors and geography and various investment strategies such as asset classes and structures. See www.rockpa.org/impactinvesting. The GIIN open access database allows investors and intermediaries to sort through over 1,000 impact investment opportunities. See www.globalimpactinvestingnetwork.org.

any rights to actively participate in the management of the fund; however, investors will have the right to vote on various fundamental matters relating to the fund and it is now commonplace for fund managers to form a limited partner advisory committee that includes key fund investors of the fund who have particular experience or whose organizations have social impact missions that are aligned with the fund's investment guidelines. Committee members provide advice to the fund managers regarding investments and also address issues such as conflicts of interests involving the fund managers on behalf of all of the fund's investors.[22]

While interest in impact investing has been growing steadily in recent years and information regarding impact investing has expanded, it is still a relatively new area and savvy investors will carefully scrutinize the experience and claims of fund managers relating to their capabilities to successfully identify and manage impact investments. One useful tool, developed for assessment of external hedge fund managers by investors but suitable for adaptation to all types of impact investment funds, is the due diligence questionnaire released by Principles for Responsible Investment (PRI) in 2017. The questionnaire includes the following questions to help investors identify fund managers that have the personnel, knowledge, and structure to incorporate ESG factors into their investment decision-making process[23]:

1. *Policy*
   1.1 Does the investment manager have a policy addressing its approach to the incorporation of ESG factors within the investment process? If yes, please provide a copy of the policy and indicate the coverage of the policy by asset class, funds, strategy, and assets under management (AUM). If there is no policy, please explain why.
   1.2 What is the investment manager's rationale for adopting a policy to incorporate responsible investment into the investment decision-making process?

---

[22] https://impact.mofo.com/funding-financing/social-impact-funds-structuring-considerations/

[23] https://unpri.org/hedge-funds/responsible-investment-ddq-for-hedge-funds/125.article

1.3 To which normative codes and initiatives is the investment manager a signatory or a voluntary adherent (e.g. the PRI, national stewardship codes, HFSB Hedge Fund Standards, CFA's Asset Manager Code of Professional Conduct, AOI Hedge Fund Principles 2014)?

2. *Governance*

2.1 Please indicate the methods of investment manager internal oversight (e.g., oversight by investment committee, firm management, board of directors, etc.), and reporting of responsible investment incorporation across the investment manager's organization.

2.2 Please describe how the investment manager has organized responsible investment responsibilities within its investment team(s) and indicate whether the investment manager employs responsible investment professionals.

2.3 Please explain what responsible investment training is provided by the investment manager to its employees.

2.4 Does the investment manager's annual employee performance review or remuneration metrics reflect any component for the inclusion of responsible investment? If yes, please describe them. If not, please explain.

3. *Investment Process*

3.1 Please describe what ESG data, research, third-party consultants, resources, tools, and practices the investment manager uses. How are these incorporated into the investment and risk management process?

3.2 Have there been any changes to the investment manager's responsible investment incorporation process over the past twelve months (e.g. additional resources, information sources)? If yes, please describe them. If not, please explain.

3.3 Please explain how active ownership practices, both voting and engagements, are integrated into investment decisions.

3.4 Please provide examples of where ESG risks and opportunities were incorporated into the investment manager's investment decisions over the past twelve months.

4. *Monitoring and Reporting*

    4.1 Please describe what metrics (internal and/or external) the investment manager uses to measure its progress in incorporating responsible investment into the investment process.

    4.2 Does the investment manager assess its fund's exposure to climate risk and measure and monitor the carbon footprint of its investment portfolio? If yes, please explain the assessment process. If not, please explain why.

    4.3 How often and in what format (e.g., meetings, written reports) does the investment manager report to its investors on ESG activities and portfolio ESG risks assessments? Please provide reporting examples.

Fund managers make their case to prospective impact investors in the various offering documents prepared when the managers begin to market their funds and then confirm their willing to meet the requirements imposed by investors in the fund's limited partnership or operating agreement and in "side letters" that include additional commitments for all of the investors or just the investors identified therein. When preparing the offering documents, fund managers need to make some fundamental decisions relating to the various questions outlined above, such as what type of environmental and social impact they are attempting to achieve, the balance to be struck between financial and impact goals and the tools that will be used to measure and report on the impact of the fund's portfolio.[24] In addition, the fund managers need to be able to differentiate their proposed fund from the growing number of competitors in the marketplace using a compelling investment and impact thesis that explains the existing need in the marketplace that will be addressed by the fund; provides credible evidence regarding the existence and extent of the need; sets out the fund's underlying theory of change; describes the proposed sectors of investment, deal size, and deal type; and demonstrates

---

[24] Private Equity Investors Embrace Impact Investing, Bain & Company (April 17, 2019), https://bain.com/insights/private-equity-investors-embrace-impact-investing/

that the projected financial and impact returns are realistic.[25] Answering these questions are essential to the success of the capital raising process, since surveys of investors conducted by the GIIN indicate that they are put off by fund managers who fail to demonstrate an understanding of the critical elements of fund structure and thoughtful consideration of terms, drivers of return, and opportunities to add value.[26]

There is no standard template for the offering documents that fund managers will use when soliciting capital from prospective investors; however, the overriding principle should be that the fund managers provide full and clear disclosure of all material facts that investors might reasonably consider when making their decisions. The offering documents should certainly describe the fund's proposed investment program and processes including the fund's specific impact theme(s), if any (e.g., affordable housing); the extent to which financial returns are the fund's sole or secondary objective; how the fund managers expect to measure and report outcomes for each impact theme (e.g., increases in the supply of affordable housing in a specific geographic region in a specific time frame); the due diligence procedures that fund managers will conduct with respect to potential investments; and the plans of the fund managers relating to management of investments and ongoing engagement with the leaders of the social enterprises that are included in the fund's investment portfolio. Specific requirements of investors regarding financial return and impact may be addressed in the offering documents and/or in the fund's partnership or operating agreement and side letters with investors. Actual and potential conflicts of interest should also be discussed include a description of how the fund managers will resolve investors' conflicting impact requirements and the circumstances under which the fund managers or their affiliates may provide services to portfolio companies. Finally, like any other offering documents, the materials for an impact

---

[25] https://thegiin.org/developing-a-private-equity-fund-foundation-and-structure/

[26] Id. Other reasons cited by investors for why fund managers fail to secure capital markets included lack of a balanced team who can execute for financial and impact returns and a substantial deal flow pipeline that indicates an ability to find good deals and deploy capital.

fund must cover the material risks of investing in the fund including the possibility of lower financial returns, execution risks associated with the new and evolving business models used by the typical portfolio companies, difficulties in measuring impact, and the shortage of reasonable exit opportunities for impact investments since they may be less likely to have strong public or secondary markets.[27]

While prospective fund managers can often prepare eloquent disclosures including processes and promises for each of the issues outlined above, investors will nonetheless look through the words to evaluate the skills and experiences of the fund managers and the team members they will be recruiting to assist in executing the impact investing strategies. Just as the investors need to address the team formation issues outlined above, fund managers need to have access to people and organizations that understand the delicate balance between achieving financial returns and generating environmental or social impact. The fund managers will typically recruit to fill various roles relating to evaluating prospective deals, negotiating the terms of investment into portfolio companies and managing the performance of those companies over the entire period of the fund's investment. The size of the team will depend on available resources and the anticipated number of deals that the fund will participate in over its life cycle, and it is common to create roles such as senior deal team leader, associate, and analyst. In addition, fund managers will often engage outside advisors and experts to provide specialized services for specific deals. When bringing people on to fill these roles, fund managers are advised to pay particular attention to skills that can be used to implement effective strategies and techniques for impact measurement and management.[28]

As for the fund managers themselves (i.e., the promoters of the fund who will be the executives of the general partner making the investment decisions and overseeing all of the team members), surveys indicate that

---

[27] Fleishhacker, E., and R. Young. 2019. "Practical Tips and Considerations for Preparing PE Impact Investment Fund Offering Documents." *Private Equity Law Report*, May 28, 2019.

[28] https://thegiin.org/developing-a-private-equity-fund-foundation-and-structure/

prospective investors are looking for a diversity of skills at the top of the organization, especially a demonstrated ability to create and manage relationships with a diverse set of key fund stakeholders including investors, entrepreneurs, directors, and executives of portfolio companies and the managers of funds that might become co-investment partners. In addition, while a successful track record as a fund manager will obviously be an important plus when marketing a new fund, investors generally give equal weight to deal and operational experience, either as a direct investor or as an entrepreneur, since the key to success as a fund manager is the ability to select and manage investments and orchestrate exit strategies. While fund managers are expected to bring in specialists to handle detailed financial analysis and accounting, they should have experience in financial management and reporting since it will be relevant to their abilities to raise funds and deploy capital. Other fund manager traits that may be important for particular investors include expertise in the fund's targeted domain and the local environment, business-building or entrepreneurial experience and demonstrated interest in and commitment to achieving social impact.

Another issue that is consistently cited as being very important to prospective investors is the ability of fund managers to credibly demonstrate that they can create a robust pipeline of investments that fit within the fund's thesis in terms of sector, stage of company and size, since the ability of investors to achieve their financial and impact goals depends heavily on finding good deals and deploying capital quickly once a fund has closed.[29] Experienced fund managers that may already be operating other funds will likely have a better sense of the pipeline because of their understanding of the needs of their current portfolio companies and their ongoing participation in the marketplace (i.e., they will already have a flow of business plans and other deal opportunities and the existing resources to vet them); however, managers starting up a new fund may have smaller networks and will obviously be focused on their own fundraising activities. Fund managers cannot commit to deals unless and until they have closed on their funds and the window for participating in a deal is often

---

[29] Id.

very narrow: companies, and other funds interested in supporting them, will not wait for fund managers to close their funds. Closing a fund usually takes a number of months and depending on the terms the fund managers will be expected to deploy most of the funds within three to five years of the final closing (a portion of the committed capital is typically reserved for follow-on investments in portfolio companies selected during the early years). In some cases, investors may commit to provide a specified amount of capital within three to four years of the fund closing but will not make those funds available until they are formally "called" by the fund managers in order to take advantage of deals that have progressed to the point where they are ready to close, thus preventing a situation where the capital sits in a money market account waiting for the fund managers to find deals.

According to guidance issued by the GIIN, fund managers looking to source deals need to both effectively market themselves and present their unique value proposition for potential investees and have a thoughtful strategy for identifying future investments (i.e., creating and maintaining an investment "pipeline").[30] Investors will scrutinize the business networks of the fund managers to assess whether they have an adequate presence in the ecosystem in which the fund proposes to operate. Among other things, fund managers should demonstrate that they have relationships with local business leaders, bankers, accountants, financial advisors, and attorneys. Fund managers should also have connections to incubators and accelerators that provide support for startups that might become suitable investment opportunities as they progress. Also important will be the ability to forge partnerships with other funds and different types of intermediaries in order to gain access to potential deals that they may have sourced and which are suitable for co-investing. The GIIN recommended that fund managers plan on spending about twelve months on sourcing a deal, starting with the time that initial contact is made with the promoters of the opportunity and then extending through due diligence and finally completing the necessary documentation to close the deal. In most cases, the fund managers will invest a significant amount of time

---

[30] Id.

investigating an opportunity only to find that it will not work out. The fund managers need to establish an internal database to track the fund's pipeline and should analyze the data regularly to identify points in the process where improvements might be made.

In addition to describing their proposed process for generating a sufficient flow of potential investment opportunities, fund managers need to be able to tell prospective investors how they intend to select the companies that will be included in the fund's investment portfolio. While investors in impact investment funds are obviously interested in potential financial returns, they need to understand how the fund managers will be evaluating and measuring the potential impact of the opportunities they are reviewing. The fund managers need to explain how impact data is collected and used to pre-screen investments, conduct due diligence and establish performance standards that can be incorporated into the terms of the investment documentation. The fund managers need to carefully document their deal selection process and formalize it so that all members of the team understand which questions need to be asked and the objective criteria that will eventually be applied to make an investment decision. A clear statement of the fund's "theory of change" is important because each investment should align with the fund's overall mission and impact goals. The fund managers should also be prepared to explain how they intend to use the fund's investment committee and will need to take into account feedback from investors regarding the role of the committee in reviewing and selecting deals and allocating resources to due diligence and others required to manage the fund's deal pipeline. In some cases, the investment committee does not get heavily involved until the parameters of a proposed transaction have been largely finalized and diligence has been completed. However, some investors prefer that the committee be brought into the process earlier and given an opportunity to compare competing opportunities that the fund managers might be considering at one time.

One issue that often gets ignored by prospective fund managers is the need for them to demonstrate to potential investors that the fund itself will be operated based on a sustainable business model that allows it to achieve its goals based on realistic assumptions, budgets, and timelines that have been developed before the fund is launched. In its guidance to fund managers, the GIIN emphasized the need for fund managers to be able to articulate a strategy for managing the key economic elements of the fund including management fees, carried interest, and capital deployment. Like any other business, fund managers need to have an economic model that takes into account the size of the fund, the type and size of investment that the fund proposes to make, projected gross returns to the fund and net returns to investors, cash flows, operating budget, and types of deal instruments that the fund will typically be using (which will influence the timing of cash flows and the risk associated with realizing the projected returns). Putting together an economic model means digging deeply into each of the elements mentioned above. For example, in order to determine the operating budget, fund managers need to determine the optimal staffing levels, which requires accurate projections about the number of prospective deals that will be evaluated over the course of the fund's lifetime and the resources that will need to be allocated to each of them.

The requirements and expectations of the investors will be set forth in a comprehensive limited partnership or operating agreement and the length of such agreements has grown steadily as the years have gone by. A good deal of space in the agreement will be devoted to provisions that are driven by the tax treatment of the entity and its owners.[31] The agreement will also cover the fund's economics (i.e., time of capital contributions, allocations of profits including the general partner's carried interest, distributions and claw backs, management fees and organizational and entity expenses); term and structure including extensions of the fund's term and the creation and use of vehicles investing alongside the fund; duties of the fund managers and other "key persons"; fund governance (i.e., fiduciary duties, cross-fund investment, co-investment allocations, advisory committee rights and processes, valuation of portfolio investments, and independent audit requirements); and financial and impact disclosures (i.e., quarterly and annual reports on financial performance,

---

[31] While the structure of limited partnership and operating agreements is relatively standard across jurisdictions, the domicile of the fund will depend on the preferences of the target investors, tax considerations and other regulatory issues such as restrictions on the flow of investment funds.

portfolio companies, and progress against impact goals). The agreement will typically be supplemented by policies relating to specific issues such as conflicts of interest and ESG reporting. Investors making the largest commitment of capital to the fund may also be afforded special rights under "side letters" between them and the fund managers covering topics such the investor's right to co-investment directly in opportunities identified by the fund managers.

When drafting the fund's limited partnership or operating agreement, particular attention should be paid to defining the scope of the fund's mission and ensuring that it includes impact-related requirements that are specific enough to facilitate meaningful measurement yet still provide the fund managers with flexibility to adjust their strategic decisions in response to changes in market conditions over the life of the fund.[32] The terms of impact-oriented funds are often longer than traditional funds (e.g., twelve years as opposed to ten, with provision for up to three additional years at the option of the fund managers to bring the full length of the term to fifteen years) because impact investments require significantly longer periods to yield acceptable returns and a longer term supports a mindset of focusing on portfolio companies that will take longer to reach profitability because of their own social missions and business models. Some funds are actually structured as "evergreen funds," which have been described as having "an indefinite lifetime in conjunction with redemption options for investors, e.g., allowing investors to opt-in or opt-out on an annual basis; allowing redemption following a formal notice process; or allowing redemption at will, with another impact investor or

---

[32] Mac Cormac, S., J. Finfrock, and B. Fox. 2019. "Impact Investing." In *The Lawyer's Corporate Social Responsibility Deskbook*, eds. A. Gutterman et al., 238. Chicago: American Bar Association. Investors will also insist that the "purposes and powers" provision of the agreement have consequences and that the agreement include remedies for material deviations from the fund's missions and procedures for determining whether a material deviation has occurred. In addition, provisions should be made for allowing tax-exempt entities that make program-related investments ("PRIs") into the fund to exit if the fund's mission changes in a way that could jeopardize the PRI's tax exemption or the tax-exempt status of the investor itself. Id.

a foundation functioning as guarantor to the fund."[33] Impact-focused funds may also use different compensation structures for the fund managers, such as distinguishing between financial and impact performance in the "carried interest" provisions (e.g., fund managers may be eligible to receive up to the traditional 20 percent carried interest; however, 15 percent might be awarded based on financial performance, and 5 percent would be awarded based on agreed measures of impact performance among the portfolio companies). Certain impact investors may also be given preferences with respect to distributions.

The use of an advisory committee consisting of representatives of the fund's investors is mentioned several times in this chapter and such a committee can serve a valuable role in providing the fund managers with access to professional investors with specialized expertise on topics central to the fund's mission and goals. Advisory committee members should be called upon to weigh in on matters that are not within the core management functions of the fund managers—selecting the fund's portfolio companies—but which are nonetheless essential for sound fund governance. Among other things, the advisory committee may be involved in review and resolution of conflicts of interest, audits of financial and impact performance and valuation of portfolio companies. The documentation for the fund will make it clear that the members of the advisory committee owe no fiduciary duties to the fund or any of its investors and that the reasonable fees and expenses of the committee will be borne by the fund.

Reports and other communications from the fund managers to the fund's investors should also be addressed in detail in the fund documents. At a minimum, investors should expect to receive quarterly and annual reports, which include financial statements for the period covered by the report and a narrative discussion of the progress of each of the fund's portfolio companies along with credible data on valuation. Financial information and valuations should be confirmed by outside auditors. In addition, the fund managers should expect to be required to provide detailed qualitative and quantitative assessments of the financial and

---

[33] Mac Cormac, S., J. Finfrock, and B. Fox. 2019. "Impact Investing." In *The Lawyer's Corporate Social Responsibility Deskbook*, eds. A. Gutterman et al., 238. Chicago: American Bar Association.

impact performance of all of the portfolio companies. Written reports should be supplemented by regular meetings between the fund managers and the investors in the fund. If possible, arrangements should be made for investors to visit the facilities of portfolio companies and meet with their managers. Good communications with the fund's investors is essential for smooth relations and building a long-term foundation that results in the investors supporting future projects of the fund managers, such as participating in new funds that the managers may decide to launch.

Fund managers should be familiar with the Private Equity Principles promulgated by the Institutional Limited Partners Association (ILPA) (https://ilpa.org/), which provide guidelines to fund managers regarding the terms that investors are likely to require in the fund documents.[34] The ILPA has made a large library of templates, standards, and model documents publicly available, all of which have been prepared in alignment with the following general principles relating to the actions of the fund managers, referred to as the "GP," and their relationship with the investors, referred to as the "LPs"[35]:

Alignment of Interest

- Alignment of interest is best achieved when the GP's wealth creation is primarily derived from a percentage of the profits generated from the GP's substantial equity commitment to the partnership, after LP return requirements have been met.

---

[34] According to its website, the ILPA engages, empowers, and connects limited partners (LPs) to maximize their performance on an individual, institutional, and collective basis and boasts of having more than 500 member institutions representing more than $2 trillion of private equity assets under management (50 percent of global institutional private equity investment). Members represent all investor categories of small and large institutions including public pensions, corporate pensions, endowments, foundations, family offices, insurance and investment companies, development financial institutions, and sovereign wealth funds.

[35] Institutional Limited Partners Association, ILPA Principles 3.0: Fostering Transparency, Governance and Alignment of Interests for General and Limited Partners (2019), 9 ("Principles in Summary").

- Decisions made by the GP, including management of conflicts of interest, should take into account the benefit to the partnership as a whole rather than to the sole or disproportionate benefit of the GP, affiliates, or a subset of investors in the partnership.
- GPs should establish and disclose written policies and procedures to identify, monitor and appropriately mitigate conflicts of interest.
- The source and value of any material benefit accruing to the GP as a consequence of being the investment manager to the partnership should be disclosed at least on an annual basis.

Transparency

- LPs should have timely access to and notifications on relevant information pertaining to the GP and management of the partnership's investments, including changes in GP ownership; material decisions and actions involving affiliates and related parties; arrangements between the GP and underlying portfolio companies; non-routine interactions with the regulator of record; material ESG matters pertaining to the portfolio; and policy violations.
- All disclosures provided to investors, including those on costs and charges, should be clear, complete, fair, and not misleading.
- Fees and expenses charged to individual LPs and the partnership as a whole, as well as carried interest calculations, should be regularly and consistently disclosed and subject to periodic review by the LP Advisory Committee (LPAC) and certification by an independent auditor.

Governance

- Fees should be reasonable and based on the normal operating costs of the fund; the partnership should not incur expenses that could rationally be expected to be covered by the management fee as a cost of operating the fund.

- GPs should neither undertake nor seek to "pre-clear" actions through overly broad disclosures that constitute or could potentially constitute a conflict of interest between the fund, a portfolio investment, and/or a portfolio manager on one hand and the GP, key persons, affiliates, etc. on the other without the approval of the LPAC.
- GPs should make an affirmative statement of the standard of care owed to the fund and should avoid language allowing for the disclaiming of fiduciary duty to the fullest extent of the law.
- LPACs should be thoughtfully constructed, mandated, and managed as an important adviser to the fund, particularly around conflicts of interest, without obligating LPAC members to serve as fiduciaries of the fund themselves.
- LPAC members should be held to minimum participation standards.
- LPAC meetings should be followed by an *in camera* session organized by the GP.

The design and structuring of impact investing funds must take into account all of the issues and concerns mentioned in the principles above; however, special consideration needs to be given to impact measurement, management, and reporting. Prospective investors will expect that the fund managers will be deploying various tools and standards to measure the impact of the fund's investment activities. In addition, fund managers should create internal structures to incentive their team members to achieve the fund's environmental and social impact goals. Fund managers should also commit to securing agreements from the managers of portfolio companies to pursue impact targets as a condition of receiving the fund's investment. The limited partnership or operating agreement should include provisions relating to impact measurement and reporting, such as a requirement that the fund managers submit written social and/or environmental impact reports to the investors, no less frequently than annually, that include at least three to five recognized impact metrics and a narrative impact report that analyzes the metrics and provides other information to investors in the form of case studies. The impact reporting should address how unforeseen outcomes from the investment activities might lead to changes in the fund's social impact thesis. Impact reporting and transparency, including sharing of data, is particularly important to investors, since many of them are just getting started in impact investing and are eager to learn from the experiences of the intermediaries in which they are participating.

While every situation is different, in general the process of designing and structuring a new fund, going out into the marketplace to find investors willing to participate in a "first close" and completing the fundraising efforts while beginning to make investments using funds collected from the first close runs between eighteen and twenty-four months. According to surveys of fund managers conducted by the GIIN, the first six months, referred to as the "First Launch" phase, including activities such as developing fund thesis and design; identifying target investors; finding an anchor investor, sponsor, or both; deciding on a placement agent; determining and establishing an operational platform; and preparing marketing materials. During the next six to twelve months, referred to by the GIIN as the "Go-to-Market" phase, the fund managers will be contacting potential investors, who will conduct a thorough vetting of the fund's operational competence and the ability of the fund managers to execute on the claims made in the fund's offering documents. Among other things, prospective investors will validate the fund's investment and impact thesis; evaluating the fund managers' strategy for achieving impact; assess the experience of the fund managers and their supporting team; visit the offices of the fund and companies in the fund's pipeline; analyze fund economics; and assess the fund's operational platform and resources. Surveys indicated that investors will closely scrutinize how fund managers act during the due diligence process, since an investment in the fund will be a long-term relationship that must be based on trust, engagement, and communication. The goal of this second phase is to get to an initial close that provides the fund with sufficient capital to make initial investments and ramp up its operational activities. Additional closing should occur within one year of the first closing and the documents generally require that fund managers must complete their fundraising within a specified period after the initial close.[36]

---

[36] https://thegiin.org/developing-a-private-equity-fund-foundation-and-structure/

CHAPTER 5

Doing the Deal

The success of an impact investor depends on its ability to access and participate in deals that allow them to deploy their capital with social enterprises that can deliver the financial and impact returns that the investor expects. As discussed in the previous chapter, fund managers must be able to demonstrate to prospective investors that they will be able to build and maintain a robust pipeline of potential investment opportunities, which will require fund managers to develop a strong profile in the marketplace and a network of contacts among the various sources of deal flow. This chapter focuses on what fund managers will need to do as they sift through their pipelines to select potential deals, conduct the necessary due diligence, complete negotiations with the founders, and other members of the executive team of the prospective portfolio companies on the economic and impact terms of the deal, finalize the legal agreements and commit the capital of their funds, and monitor and supervise the progress of the enterprises up to the point where it is appropriate for the fund to exit the investment. Selection, due diligence, and negotiation all take time, usually nine to twelve months, and once the deal is completed the fund should expect to be actively engaged in monitoring for three to five years, perhaps more, depending on the portfolio company's stage of development at the time that the initial investment is made. In many cases, the fund will make a "follow-on" investment in a subsequent round of funding. Clearly, the fund and its portfolio companies will have a long-term relationship and what happens while they are "doing the deal" will be important in laying the foundation for mutual success.

Deal Selection

As noted above, a large pipeline of potential investments is important for fund managers and surveys indicated that established funds may have literally hundreds of prospective portfolio companies in their databases at any point in time. However, quantity is no substitute for quality and the fund managers need to implement screening mechanisms to weed out opportunities that are not aligned with the fund's impact goals and objectives and, for those deals that survive the initial screening, identify key issues that will need to explored and resolved during due diligence in order for the fund to make a commitment. Surveys illustrate how demanding and difficult the selection process can be—for example, from the initial group of companies that have been placed into the fund's pipeline during the run-up to the fund's initial close and the months following the close, perhaps 25 percent will turn out to be a good fit the fund's investment strategy and only half of those prospects will be selected for additional review due to resource limitations within the fund (e.g., the available time of the fund managers and their internal team). Only 20–25 percent of those companies will survive the additional review, which will include close scrutiny of impact data available from a review of the business plans offered by the promoters of the target companies, to move into the due diligence phase and of those companies it is likely that the fund may ultimately invest in 50–80 percent of them.[1]

If you do the math on the selection process outlined above it is clear that only a few companies—usually somewhere around 2 percent of all that started—will survive and end up in the fund's portfolio. Not all investment opportunities are suitable, even if they ultimately turn out to be "successful" by some measure, and the decision for the fund managers will be based on their specific strategies, impact goals and objectives, and risk tolerance, among other things. According to the GIIN, some basic factors that fund managers should consider in their initial screening include the following[2]:

- For sponsors or owners, who are the driving forces and what are their motivations for managing the business?
- What is the market opportunity for the business?
- Can the company deliver its products or services efficiently?

---

[1] https://thegiin.org/developing-a-private-equity-fund-foundation-and-structure/ (Figure 11: Filtering the Investee Pipeline)

[2] Id.

- How is the company organized?
- Does the company operate transparently?
- Does this investment align with fund mission or impact objectives (ideally grounded in an organizational theory of change)?
- How is the company currently performing toward impact goals? Can it optimize for higher impact?

The fund managers bear the ultimate responsibility for the choices made during the deal selection process; however, as discussed in the previous chapter, it is common for funds to provide for the creation of an investment committee that includes representatives from the key investors in the fund who are available to provide input to the fund managers on the companies that are included in the fund's portfolio and, as requested, the specific terms of particular transactions. The role of the investment committee, and the requirements of investment committee members regarding information and participation, will vary depending on the circumstances. In many cases, the investment committee will convene several times during the deal process, beginning with the point where decisions are made about which opportunities will move forward into due diligence and then picking up again when the due diligence is completed and it is time for the fund managers to negotiate the terms of investment and prepare and sign the transactional documents. Earlier involvement by the investment committee means that it will have more input into the design of the portfolio, but some investment committee members prefer to limit their participation to reviewing proposals that have already been vetted by the fund managers and their team, thus relying on the fund managers to do the hard work of sifting through the blizzard of potential deals that occurs when the fund is first formed.

Investment Criteria of Sustainable Investors

Sustainable investors are concerned not only with what companies are striving to accomplish, but also with the way in which those companies intend to operate and the values and methods that will be used by the principals of the companies. Specifically, sustainable investors look for individuals and companies that value and exhibit transparency and honesty and candor in communications among stakeholders; define economic success by social and ecological impact, not just financial results; have an entrepreneurial spirit and culture that encourages and fosters innovation and continuous improvement; and which are truly pioneers in their areas interested in building the fields in which they operate through collaboration and "open sourcing" of methods and ideas. Sustainable investors also tend to be particularly interested in developing and maintaining close, long-term relationships with their investees and providing them with appropriate support and resources throughout the investment period. One way this is accomplished is by matching entrepreneurs with local investors from the same community to develop a sense of shared responsibility and facilitate face-to-face interaction.

Enterprises seeking financing from social venture capital funds and other sustainable investors need to understand the criteria that these types of investors use when evaluating potential portfolio companies. A modest survey of the published investment criteria of various investors indicates that are looking for companies that:

- Have a primary, clear objective to achieve significant social change and a business model in which generating social impact is an essential and necessary part.
- Provide goods and services that meet human needs and have significant social impact (e.g., food, medicine, clothing, housing, heat and light, transportation, communication, recreation, renewable energy, and "green" products and services). These goods or services must be based on core technology that is economically better or create greater social impact than what is available currently through the market, aid, or charitable distribution. Sustainable investors prefer and expect evidence of customer feedback on the utility of the proposed goods or services.
- Have a clear business plan and model that demonstrates the potential for financial viability and sustainability

within a five to seven year period, including the ability
to cover operating expenses with operating revenues and
generate a fair return for investors.

- Have a strong and experienced management team with
the skills, will, and vision to execute the business plan, an
unwavering commitment to achieving the desired social
impact in an ethical manner.

- Demonstrate a clear path to scale for the number of end
users over the anticipated investment period, and be
positioned as one of the leaders in the market.

- Provide positive leadership in the areas of business operations and overall activities that are material to improving
societal outcomes, including those that will affect future
generations.

- Balance the needs of financial and nonfinancial stakeholders and demonstrate a commitment to the global commons
as well as to the rights of individuals and communities.

- Advance environmental sustainability and resource
efficiency by reducing the negative impact of business
operations on the environment, managing water scarcity
and ensuring efficient and equitable access to clean sources,
mitigating impact on all types of natural capital, dimin-
ishing climate-related risks and reducing carbon emissions, and driving sustainability innovation and resource
efficiency through business operations and products and
services. Red flags for sustainable investors would include
a record of poor environmental performance and failure to
comply with applicable laws and regulations, activities that
contribute significantly to local or global environmental
problems, and/or risks related to the operation of nuclear
power facilities.

- Establish an environmental management system with
objectives and procedures for evaluating progress, minimizing negative impacts, training personnel, and trans-
ferring best practices to customers, suppliers, and other

participants in the marketplace through trade associations and other collaborations.

- Contribute to the quality of human and animal life. Sustainable investors will not invest in companies that abuse animals, cause unnecessary suffering and death of animals, or whose operations involve the exploitation or mistreatment of animals.
- Contribute to the community through charitable giving, encouraging employee volunteering in the community, making products and services available free or at cost to community groups and supporting local suppliers and striving to hire locally.
- Respect consumers by marketing products and services in a fair and ethical manner, maintaining integrity in customer relations, and ensuring the security of sensitive consumer data.
- Respect human rights, respect culture and tradition in local communities and economies, and respect Indigenous Peoples' Rights. Sustainable investors will not invest in companies that have exhibited a pattern and practice of human rights violations or have been directly complicit in human rights violations committed by governments or security forces.
- Promote diversity and gender equity across workplaces, marketplaces, and communities. Sustainable investors look for diversity throughout the organization, beginning with the board and senior management team, and will not invest in companies that discriminate on the basis of race, age, ethnicity, religion, gender, sexual orientation, or perceived disability or support the discriminatory activities of others in their workplaces, marketplaces, or communities. Red flags include a record of consistent violations of workplace-related laws and regulations and failure to adopt and enforce explicit policies against discrimination in hiring, salary, promotion, training, or termination of employment.

- Demonstrate a commitment to employees by ensuring development, communication, appropriate economic opportunity and decent workplace standards. Sustainable investors will not invest in companies that have been singled out for serious labor-related actions or penalties by regulatory agencies or that have demonstrated a pattern of employing forced, compulsory or child labor. Sustainable investors seek confirmation that companies have implemented and follow personnel policies that promote the welfare of their employees, adhere to internationally recognized labor standards, value employee welfare and safety, pay a living wage to its employees, and maintain a reasonable ratio of CEO earnings to average employee earnings, maintain cordial and professional relations with labor unions, and bargain fairly with their employees, and follow sustainable employment practices.
- Save lives by guaranteeing product safety while promoting public health. Concerns for safety and public health caused sustainable investors to reject proposals from companies engaged in certain "prohibited business activities" such as the manufacture and/or sale of tobacco products; the manufacture of alcoholic beverages or gambling operations; the manufacture and/or sale firearms and/or ammunition; or manufacture, design, or sale of weapons or the critical components of weapons that violate international humanitarian law.
- Provide responsible stewardship of capital in shareholders' best interests.
- Exhibit accountable governance and develop effective boards that reflect expertise and diversity of perspective and provide oversight of sustainability risk and opportunity. Sustainable investors will shun companies that have demonstrated poor governance, including failure to practice transparency in disclosures to shareholders or respond to shareholder communications or proposals, or engaged in harmful or unethical business practices.

- Commit to an external code or standard or a set of business principles that provides a framework to measure the company's progress on environmental and social issues.
- Integrate environmental and social risks, impacts, and performance in their material financial disclosures in order to inform shareholders, benefit stakeholders, and seek their ideas and views and contribute to company strategy.
- Lift ethical standards in all operations, including in dealings with customers, regulators, and business partners. Sustainable investors require that the companies in which they invest adopt and rigorously follow codes of conduct that are based on recognized global best practices to guide their policies, programs, and operations.
- Demonstrate transparency and accountability in addressing adverse events and controversies while minimizing risks and building trust.

Sustainable investors often focus their activities on companies engaged in addressing needs, problems, and challenges in a specific societal domain and/or geographic area. Popular target societal domains include agriculture, education, safety, demography, community, poverty, environment, health and well-being, housing, and ethical goods and services. Geographic areas that have attracted substantial interest from sustainable investors include East Africa, West Africa, India, Pakistan, and Latin America.

Given the nature of some of the requirements described above, it is not surprising that many sustainable investors are not interested in pure "startups" and are looking for companies that have advanced to the "early stage" of development and have identified a stable business model that has already achieved some minimum level of revenues.

Many sustainable investors have developed "exclusionary criteria" that list activities and other characteristics that will disqualify companies from investment consideration. For example, a sustainable investor is quite likely to rule out funding companies that:

- Are involved in the extraction of carbon based resources, such as coal, petroleum, and natural gas, for the production of fossil fuels;
- Are primarily involved in producing or distributing alcohol or tobacco products;
- Develop, manufacture, or profit from weapons, including conventional, chemical, biological, and nuclear weapons;
- Generate nuclear power;
- Genetically modify seeds or living organisms (although such activities may be allowed with a showing of countervailing social benefits such as demonstrating leadership in promoting safety, protection of Indigenous Peoples' Rights, the interests of organic farmers, and the interests of developing countries generally);
- Are involved in the gambling, gaming, or adult entertainment industries;
- Have primary business practices that involve the inhumane treatment of animals; or
- Have profited from conspicuous consumption, land speculation, predatory financial practices, or privatized detention facilities.

Source: The criteria identified and discussed in the text draws upon a review of published criteria of various social venture firms and investors including Calvert Group, Acumen Fund, City Light Capital, and Root Capital. Each investor has its own specific set of requirements based on its goals and objectives. For links to information on other social venture capital firms, see Cause Capitalism "15 Social Venture Capital Funds That You Should Know About," http://causecapitalism.com/15-social-venture-capital-firms-that-you-should-know-about/#sthash.A7KQmImG.dpuf

Due Diligence

Careful selection of potential deal opportunities should bring the fund managers to the point where they can devote their resources, and the skills and experience of their team managers, to conducting comprehensive due diligence on the prospective portfolio companies and their managers. Due diligence is arguably one of the most important activities that the fund managers will undertake and a solid process of conducting due diligence should be in place before it all begins. According to the GIIN, due diligence serves a number of important purposes: including as a risk management tool, an opportunity to identify ways to add value to and improve the impact of an investee, a way to identify the social or environmental impact, or both, of the business, and a means to respond to the expectations of the fund's investors.

In order to realize the benefits of due diligence, consideration must be given to the key elements identified by the GIIN[3]:

- Current, historical, and projected financial performance
- Overall business strategy and market position and environment
- Overall impact strategy
- Financial management strategy
- Operating efficiencies and inefficiencies
- Potential externalities
- Integrity and background checks for sponsors, owners, and managers
- Potential financial, environmental, and social risks analysis
- Legal due diligence
- Governance structure and company management
- Opportunities for growth and improvement

There is no universal standard for conducting due diligence and the sequencing of the focus on particular elements depends on the preferences of the fund managers and the availability of information from the prospective investees. In most cases, several elements will be investigated

---

[3] Id. (Figure 13: Important Elements of Due Diligence) See also McCreless, M. 2014. "Social & Environmental Due Diligence: From the Impact Case to the Business Case." *Root Capital*, (https://rootcapital.org/resources/social-environmental-due-diligence-from-the-impact-case-to-the-business-case/)

simultaneously and the due diligence will require request and review of documents, completion of questionnaires, interviews and inspections, and inquiries of the company's business partners. In addition to the fund's internal team, due diligence may also be conducted by outside professionals such as attorneys, accountants, and consultants with expertise in a specific sector and familiarity with the techniques associated with impact measurement.

Risk Management

The limited partner investors in a fund rely on the fund managers to identify, manage, and mitigate the risks associated with the deployment of their capital, assuming that the fund managers are better placed to fulfill those responsibilities as a result of their experience and the resources that they have collected in putting together their team. Risks should be assessed in a number of ways during the due diligence process and the results of the risk analysis should be used to determine whether to proceed with an investment and, if so, how the investment should be structured in order to fit within the risk profile that the fund managers have presented to their investors. The first step is to identify all of the risks associated with the prospective portfolio company, which can include macro, market, human resources, products, operations, financial, and ESG, and assess the company's ownership and financial structure (e.g., how is ownership and financial distribution preferences already allocated among debt and equity holders, as well as outside lenders). Once the risks have been identified and quantified, the fund managers can take steps to mitigate the risks through the choice of the investment instrument, pricing and creating options for exiting the investment (either completely or through conversion into another form of investment instrument with different risk characteristics). Another strategy is the fund managers to condition the fund's investment on certain risk mitigation actions by the portfolio company, such as purchasing insurance to cover a specific potential risk.[4]

---

[4] https://thegiin.org/developing-a-private-equity-fund-foundation-and-structure/ (Figure 14: Managing Risk)

Adding Value

The due diligence phase is the first time that the fund managers have an opportunity to interact directly with the founders and executive team members of the prospective portfolio companies and the all parties should use this as an opportunity to develop a foundation for the fund managers adding value to the business, assuming that an investment is eventually made. For example, if potential problems are discovered during the due diligence, actions will certainly need to be taken to resolve them or mitigate their impact in order for the fund managers to be comfortable with proceeding. However, the fund managers can facilitate this process by making specific suggestions to the leaders of the company and perhaps introducing consultants and other resource providers who can offer specialized assistance. The fund managers may also provide input on possible changes to the company's business model and strategies that will improve its overall financial and impact performance. In addition, certain requirements imposed by the fund managers at the behest of their own investors, such as expanded impact measurement and reporting, will also lead to improvements in the company's transparency and its ability to communicate to other stakeholders. Depending on the situation and the investment terms that are eventually negotiated, one of the fund managers may join the company's board of directors, providing him or her with a direct and formal role in the stewardship of the company. The due diligence phase is an opportunity for everyone to see whether that sort of relationship would be workable. Even if the fund does not have a representative on the board, its fund managers should be comfortable that they will have access to the management team to provide counseling and share experience and expertise.

Identifying and Measuring Impact

Investors considering placing their capital with the managers of traditional venture capital and private equity funds certainly expect those managers to carefully analyze the business and financial models of prospective portfolio companies to determine a reasonable risk-adjusted financial return on investment. When it is intended that the fund engage in impact investing, another layer of review is added: identifying and measuring the environmental and/or social impact that can be expected from an investment in a portfolio company. An initial impact screening should occur well before companies are selected for the more intense due diligence phase and fund managers should create an "impact committee" that includes members of the internal team and experts recommended by the fund's investors to focus specifically on the proposed impact thesis and theory of change for each of the companies that the fund managers are considering moving forward to due diligence. At this stage, since due diligence has not started, the group will have relatively limited information on how the company is actually performing; however, the impact committee can compare the company's business model to the fund's own impact goals and critically review the projections made by the company regarding growth and projected impact and the company's assumptions regarding risks and challenges. If the company's business plan raises too many questions, the fund managers may pass on the opportunity. On the other hand, if the impact proposition of the company is solid and the assumptions are reasonable, it may be moved forward into more extensive financial due diligence. In close cases, the fund managers may request additional impact-related information from the company before committing to full-blown due diligence. Another output of this process is ideas that the fund managers can provide to the company on improving their messaging and strategies relating to impact.[5]

Investor Expectations

The primary goal of the due diligence process is to make the best decisions regarding the deployment of the capital provided by fund's investors to the fund managers. Once an investment is made in a portfolio company, it cannot easily be undone. If adverse information about the company comes to the attention of the fund managers after a deal is closed, the fund may have legal rights; however, this is not a productive path for

---

[5] The GIIN has assembled a list of various resources that fund managers can use to integrate impact considerations into their investment management including The Impact Management Project, Navigating Impact Project, IRIS and the Impact Toolkit. Id.

any of the parties. As such, the fund's investors will expect that the fund managers will put in place a comprehensive and professional process for both financial and impact due diligence that is clearly aligned with the issues and best practices in the sectors in which the fund will be operating. The scope of the due diligence should also demonstrate a recognition and understanding of the specific risks and operational issues that are most commonly found among the typical target portfolio companies. The fund managers should create and maintain a record of the due diligence investigation for each of the portfolio companies and be prepared to share with the fund's investors how they identified and managed potential risks and the steps that they are taking to monitor issues that may have been identified during the process (including covenants for post-closing actions by the company and its management included in the deal documents).

Company's Due Diligence on Prospective Investors

An integral feature of sustainable entrepreneurship and corporate social responsibility is ensuring that the resources required to establish and operate the business are sourced in a responsible manner that does not impair the integrity and reputation of the company. While transparency regarding sources of funding is relatively robust among public companies, which are subject to extensive reporting requirements imposed by governments and securities exchanges, the same is far from true in the startup world and the risks for sustainable entrepreneurs are increasing as rogue investors dangle capital in front of them at the same time as employees, customers, and other stakeholders demand that founders be able to explain how their businesses are funded. Founders need to understand the techniques they can use to conduct due diligence on prospective investors and ask questions to prospective business partners to determine how they are funded and the pressures they may be under from their own investors.

The robust economic conditions during the mid-2010s have encouraged many fledgling venture capitalists to hit the road to attract capital for their initial funds and they have often been advised to go after so-called "easy money": billions of dollars available from sovereign wealth funds managed by Middle Eastern countries such as Saudi Arabia and Abu Dhabi looking to become major players in Silicon Valley and other innovation clusters around the United States and in Europe. The strategy seemed to make sense and, in fact, appeared to have been endorsed by major investment players such as SoftBank, an investor in Uber and other high-profile Silicon Valley companies that had accepted a commitment of $45 billion from Saudi Arabia's Public Investment Fund. However, even before news of additional repressive political tactics in those countries came to light in 2018, fund managers, increasingly sensitive to calls for responsible investment, were hesitant about taking money tied to those countries and were instead focusing their fundraising on wealthy individuals, nonprofit organizations, universities, and pension funds committed to conforming to international standards for investing in an environmentally and socially responsible manner.[6]

More and more investors must now contend with questions from founders and executives of their existing portfolio companies, as well as questions during the courting process with prospective funding targets, about where the money they are investing came from. In particular, founders are asking investors whether they have received money from sources that are connected to foreign governments with poor human rights records or from foreign investors looking to effectively "launder" profits from illegal and unethical business activities in their home countries. Another concern is funding from government-supported sources in countries such as China and Russia where there are significant risks that one of the purposes of the investment is to gain access to proprietary technology and strategic business information. Venture capital firms have traditionally been less than forthcoming about their own investors (they are under no legal obligation to disclose the information, often keep it secret for competitive reasons and may actually refuse funding from public pension funds that publish the results of their investments); however, it is becoming clear they may often not have a clear idea about where the money is coming from because they have failed to ask the right questions themselves and/or investors employ sophisticated schemes such as shell companies to mask where the funds are actually controlled.

---

[6] Griffith, E. 2018. "Suddenly Questioning Easy Money For Start-Ups." *The New York Times*, November 3, 2018, B1.

Some founders, with the support of their investors, have extended their concerns about financial and business support from repressive regimes beyond investors to include partnerships with customers, distributors, and suppliers, announcing that they would not do business with companies that have taken money from such regimes and/or conduct significant amounts of business with affiliates of such regimes. Companies are also concerned about doing business with firms that have board members designated by "questionable" investors since sensitive details of transactions are often distributed and discussed at directors' meetings. In addition, lack of clarity about ownership and control of investment vehicles means that a founder may discover that one of its investors has also provide capital to competitors through affiliates as part of a broader scheme to gain access to the details of all proprietary technology relevant to a particularly promising sector regardless of which companies own that technology or whether any specific company will be most successful.

Investors have always conducted extensive due diligence on the founders of prospective portfolio companies and their proposed business models, seeking information on the company's governance, management, and finances and often meeting with customers, distributions, suppliers, and other business partners; however, the founders themselves have rarely asked too many questions about potential investors, perhaps fearing that aggressive "reverse due diligence" would cause investors to back away. However, experts caution founders about being too timid, noting that the relationship with an equity investor is akin to a marriage that cannot easily be undone and thus must be entered into only if and when there is trust on both sides. Recommendations for reverse due diligence provide by one experienced adviser to founders include getting a perspective from peer investors; personally visiting another startup funded by the investor; doing research on investor visibility via Google and social media; inviting the investor to dinner or a fun-related activity; and conducting a routine credit and background check.[7] In addition, founders need to be direct

---

and clear about asking investors to explain the source of the funds that are to be invested and not be satisfied with vague and elusive answers.

Selecting the Investment Instrument

As the fund manager completes the due diligence process and moves toward a decision about whether or not to invest in a particular company, consideration must also be given to selecting the investment instrument and negotiating the specific terms of the instrument relating to the use of the funds, distributions, preferences, or subordination in relation to the company's other financing instruments and exit mechanisms. Each side has its own interests to consider in selecting the investment instrument and the fund managers will obviously need to take into account the expectations of the fund's investors as to the types of instruments the fund will be including in its portfolio. As discussed in a previous chapter, the parties must determine whether the investment will take the form of debt or equity. Debt, of course, means that the fund will be lending money to the portfolio company with the expectation that the principal amount will be returned in full by a specific maturity date. Equity financing involves selling the fund an ownership interest in the business. There are positive and negative aspects to each type of financing. The cost to the company of each type of funding is different, as is the way they are treated for tax purposes. The interest on borrowed money is deductible by a business for tax purposes, which reduces the effective cost to the company. Dividends that might be paid on the same investment in stock would typically not be tax deductible by the company. In selling stock there usually is no firm commitment to pay the money back but the fund will insist on extensive contractual rights to have a voice in the management of the company. Financing may also be structured as a combination of debt and equity when appropriate to fit the specific needs of the company.

Funds vary significantly in their preferences regarding the types of investment instruments that they purchase. For example, funds may specialize in investing through fixed income securities, typically debt instruments, or equity securities that are traded in public markets. The discussion in this chapter focuses on impact investment funds following a strategy similar to traditional venture capital funds, which means that the capital will be deployed through equity financing (including debt instruments that can be readily converted into equity securities upon satisfaction of certain conditions). When assessing an investment in a company that is in its early stages of development, fund managers generally consider the following types of instruments[8]:

- *Convertible Notes*: Convertible notes are frequently used for early-stage financings and should be thought of as debt securities (i.e., including principal amounts due at a maturity date, accrued interest provisions, and a claim on the company's assets as an unsecured creditor (although in rare instances a convertible note will also be "secured"). It is intended that the notes will eventually, prior to the maturity date, convert into the same preferred equity security that the company issues in its first round of equity financing to a larger and more sophisticated group of investors, often referred to as the "Series A round" because the company will be issuing Series A preferred stock. The terms of that conversion will depend on provisions negotiated by the company and the noteholders, including a discount rate and a valuation cap. Provisions are also included to address what happens in the even the company is sold prior to a Series A round and what happens if the notes remain outstanding on the maturity date (i.e., the company failed to close its Series A round as scheduled). Not all impact investors are willing to invest using convertible notes, preferring to wait until the company has matured to the point where it is able to attract sufficient interest among investors to raise money in a Series A round.
- *Preferred Stock*: The holders of preferred stock have preferences over the other shareholders with regard to distributions in the form of dividends and upon the occurrence of certain "liquidity events" such as the sale or dissolution of the company. Distributions on preferred shares may be tied to a fixed schedule or the achievement of certain milestones relating to the

---

[8] Adapted from 2017. *Startup Seed Financings: Overview*. New York, NY: Thomson Reuters Practice Law Corporate and Securities.

company's business. Impact investment funds typically prefer "convertible preferred stock," which provides the holders with protections and superior rights in relation to common shares but also the opportunity to realize a larger return on their investment by converting their preferred shares into common shares when a market for the common shares emerges (i.e., upon the occurrence of an initial public offering). When convertible preferred shares are issued to impact investors, the company will grant additional rights to the investors in the charter documents and by contract including information rights, rights to vote on and approve certain matters as a separate group, registration rights, rights of first refusal and co-sale, price-based anti-dilution provisions, drag-along rights, and rights to designate a representative on the board of directors.[9]

- *SAFEs (Simple Agreement for Future Equity)*: Safes were developed as a company-friendly alternative to convertible notes that have the same conversion features of notes (and the same variables to consider, such as discount rate and valuation cap) without a maturity date or interest accrual. Safes seem to be more prevalent among "hot" deals where investors are scrambling to be included and have less leverage to negotiate more protections like those normally seen in convertible

---

[9] The terms of the convertible preferred stock described in the text are generally associated with so-called "Series A Preferred Stock", an important steps in a company's development. It should be noted, however, that companies may issue some form of convertible preferred stock, rather than the convertible notes described above, in the later stages of seed financing and/or when the size of the financing is relatively large and the investor group is experienced and sophisticated and each investing fairly large amounts of money (i.e., over $100,000 per investor). The instrument is often referred to as "Series Seed Preferred Stock" and will include several of the same protections and rights afforded to investors in the Series A round such as information rights and rights to vote separately on certain actions proposed by the founders as common stockholders. At the same time, Series Seed Preferred Stock typically does not include some of the more complex terms seen in Series A rounds and the liquidation rights of Series Seed Preferred are typically limited to a return of the purchase price before distributions are made to common stockholders, with a right to convert to common stock and waive the liquidation preference.

notes. Safes were developed to provide a quick and low-cost solution to seed financing, and this can be accomplished if investors understand what they are buying. Investors seeking some protections or rights while accepting a safe can bargain for information rights, rights of first refusal, and so on, to be included in a side letter.

- *Common Stock*: While not frequently used for raising capital from impact investors during the early stages of development, companies can issue common stock, which is the same security that will be held by the founders and employees of the company and subordinated to government claims or taxes, regulated employee claims (e.g., pension obligations), all trade and bank debt and any preferred shares issued by the company. The main reason for using common stock is simplicity and relatively low legal costs. However, while investors issued common stock can be given voting rights and rights to receive dividends and distribution on liquidation, they would generally not have the same rights, preferences, and privileges given to later round investors unless those are negotiated separately, which would increase the cost of issuing the common stock. Moreover, issuing common stock significantly complicates valuation of those types of shares for equity incentive purposes. All in all, common stock has drawbacks for both sides of the transaction—founders and investors—and it is therefore unlikely that common shares will be used for early-stage impact investments.

When considering companies that have passed through the early stages of development (and have perhaps already issued one of the forms of instruments discussed above, such as a Series A round), impact investors may invest through different types of instruments including the following[10]:

- *Participating Loan:* The investor makes a loan to the company on terms which provide that payments to the investor will

---

[10] https://thegiin.org/developing-a-private-equity-fund-foundation-and-structure/

be based on the company's profits over the term of the loan. In some cases, the parties will also agree that the investor will be entitled to fixed-interest payments that are not tied to profitability.

- *Equity-Like Debt:* Equity-like debt is similar to the convertible notes described above, but with more elaborate covenants. Often referred to as "bonds," the holders have the right to convert into equity securities of the company or cash of equal value at an agreed-upon price and up to a specified expiration date. Interest payments during the term of the bond may be required to mitigate the investor's risk, with the amount and timing depending on the company's stage of development and ability to service the payments. In lieu of the conversion feature, investors may be issued a warrant, which is a security that provides the holder with the right to purchase equity securities at a preagreed exercise price (either by tendering cash or surrendering the bond as consideration for the exercise) until the expiration date of the warrant.

- *Mezzanine Finance:* Mezzanine financing is a combination of debt and equity financing used by companies that have already taken on debt financing from commercial lenders that have taken a senior position with respect to security interests in the company's assets. Since the investor's rights are necessarily junior to the senior lenders (but senior to claims of equity holders), it bargains for a financial return that is higher than that of the senior lenders (but still lower than a pure equity investment) including a higher interest rate and rights to convert into equity. Common forms of mezzanine finance include subordinated loans, participating loans, convertible bonds, and bonds with warrants.

Deal Terms

The terms of the deal should align the financial, strategic, and impact goals of the company to those of the fund and should be based on strong and clear communications between the fund managers and the company's management team. The deal terms will vary depending on the form of investment instrument that is used, debt or equity, the requirements of the investors, the stage of the company's development and the terms upon which the company has previously raised capital (including loans from commercial lenders). The key issues for the parties generally involve the duration of the investment (repayment of a loan or mandatory redemption of an equity investment); payments over the term of the investment, such as interest payments on a loan or dividends on equity securities, which may be tied to various measures of performance; preferences upon liquidation of the business or the sale of the company; voting rights including the right to vote separately on specified transactions; rights to convert the instrument into different securities of the company; and covenants relating to the use of funds and other operational activities of the company. The GIIN recommends that investors work with the managers of their prospective portfolio companies to set impact goals and expectations; define evidence-based investment strategies that target specific environmental and/or social problems such as affordable housing or clean energy; select metrics and establish targets using generally accepted tools such as IRIS; and measure, track, use the data and report.[11]

Burand noted impact investors have experimented with a number of structure and investment terms in an effort to align the timing and amount of their financial returns from investment in portfolio companies with the business models of those companies. Examples offered by Burand based on the results of extensive studies of innovative deal structures for debt and equity impact investments, as well as grants, included[12]:

- Grant funders developed "repayable grant" facilities that, upon the occurrence of certain agreed milestones, often

---

[11] https://thegiin.org/developing-a-private-equity-fund-foundation-and-structure/

[12] Burand, D. 2015. "Resolving Impact Investment Disputes: When Doing Good Goes Bad." *Washington University Journal of Law & Policy* 48, no. 55, 61–63, https://openscholarship.wustl.edu/law_journal_law_policy/vol48/iss1/9 (citing D. Propper de Callejon et al., Innovative Deal Structures for Impact Investments (2014) (report) (on file with author)).

operational or financial targets, converted their grants into loans that the grant recipient was expected to repay to the donor.

- Some lenders offered borrowers more flexible repayment schedules by rejecting a traditional fixed payment schedule in favor of variable payment structures that were triggered only if and when the borrower achieved certain thresholds of revenues or cash flows.

- Lenders also provided generous amortization schedules, lengthening the periods to ten years of more, offered grace periods of eighteen to twenty-four months before any payments on their loans were required and agreed to forego prepayment penalties or, in a few cases, offer prepayment discounts.

- Impact investors deployed a "demand dividend" structure that did not guarantee dividends to the investors but established a formula for variable payments that included the following features: (1) a payment schedule that is tied to the cash flow of the investee, (2) a honeymoon period (grace period) where repayment obligations are deferred, (3) a fixed payment obligation that is calculated as a multiple of the amount lent to the investee, and (4) covenants focused on ensuring that the investee reached and maintained a positive cash flow.

Another strategy that is used by impact investors in monitoring the activities of their portfolio companies through provisions in the deal documents is the use of covenants. For example, investors may require specific language in the documents regarding the steps that the company will take to ensure that its operational activities are consistent with the expectations of all parties regarding the company's social impact and its relationships with the ultimate beneficiaries (e.g., consumers or community members). In situations where the company will be providing underserved communities with access to financial services, the impact investors will require not only that the company comply with all applicable laws and regulations, but also demonstrate that it has provided clear and comprehensive information to all of its customers. The impact investors will also demand that the company refrain from unfair or harmful debt collection practices. Impact investors also commonly insist on detailed reporting provisions that obligate portfolio companies to provide quantitative and qualitative information on the social impact of their operations.[13]

The Impact Terms Guide, a joint project of the Introduction to Social Entrepreneurship course at Harvard Law School and the Impact Terms Platform, focused on how to incorporate the broad principles and practices applied in impact investing into the agreements used to document the terms of an impact investment.[14] The Impact Terms Platform also includes a library of case studies and term sheets that can be consulted for other strategies that might be used in drafting impact-related terms for investment documents.[15] With regard to incorporating requirements on enterprises in investment documents relating to tracking "quantified impact" the Impact Terms Guide suggested several approaches:

- Obligation to develop a formal program to measure impact in order to ensure that measurement is sustainable and transparent using language such as the following: "The Company must develop a program to measure impact in partnership with the Investor, utilizing available tools such as IRIS, GIIRS, or other tools mutually agreed upon by both parties." or "The Company must develop a program to measure social impact according to the 'IRIS' methodology and indicators, including two visits per year. The Company must also get certified by GIIRS as a GIIRS Rated Company."

- Obligation to regularly notify/report on relevant impact metrics to the investor using language such as the following: "No more than thirty (30) days after the end of each quarterly accounting period, the Company shall notify the Investor in writing information on the state of the business, including total employment metrics, key performance metrics, and other measures of impact, plus non-quantitative information

---

[13] Id. at 64.

[14] https://impactterms.org/impact-terms-guide/

[15] https://impactterms.org/case-studies-term-sheets/

inclusive of major accomplishments and major lessons learned."[16]

- Obligation to regularly deliver social and environmental impact reports using language such as the following: "At least once a year, the Company shall submit a written social and/or environmental impact report that includes a minimum of 3–5 impact metrics (which must include reporting on the number of underserved entrepreneurs funded (including by race, gender, age), number of funded companies located in an economically distressed or disadvantaged area, amounts invested originally and as follow-on funding, and number of low-income individuals employed) which will be based whenever possible on existing reporting metrics and practices and which will incorporate IRIS metrics, as feasible and appropriate."[17]

- Obligation to obtain third-party verification of the company's impact reporting using language such as the following: "Each impact report required to be delivered to the Investor

---

[16] The language on reporting on relevant impact metrics would be in addition to the requirements for providing customary information rights including audited annual financial statements, unaudited quarterly and semi-annual financial statements, cash flow statements and reports on usage of funds, quarterly commercial report in the specified format detailing the commercial progress made by the company with respect to its main KPIs and an annual budget. Specific dates for delivery of each of these reports will also need to be determined and specified, such as requiring that audited financial statements be delivered within 90 or 120 days of the end of the relevant fiscal year and that the business plan be delivered no later than 30 days prior to the beginning of the next fiscal year.

[17] The Impact Terms Guide recommended that written narrative impact reports should contain details relating to the social and/or environmental impact of the company's activities including analysis of impact metrics, anecdotes related to the impact of the company's activities, case studies, changes in social impact thesis or criteria, and other related impact outputs and outcomes. In addition, the Impact Terms Guide called for reports to contain detailed explanations of the company's policies and activities in relation to ESG matters and in the absence of such systems, a clear and reasonable explanation for not doing so or steps being undertaken to put such policies in place. The report should contain analysis about how much change occurred as a result of those policies and activities.

hereunder shall be audited by a third-party organization with relevant expertise, selected by the Investor and reasonably acceptable to the Company. Costs of the audit shall be borne by the Company. If mutually agreed, the findings of the audit may be publicized by the Investor and the Company."[18]

- Obligation to regularly complete impact certifications based on a reputable third-party impact assessment and rating system using language such as the following: "The Company hereby agrees to complete an impact certification on behalf of the Global Impact Investing Rating System (GIIRS) at least once annually post-Closing."[19]

With regard to incorporating "specific purpose" into investment documents the Impact Terms Guide suggested several approaches[20]:

- Include a social investment purpose covenant to express to all parties involved that the investment is being made with specific purposes in mind in addition to monetary gains using language such as the following: "The social purpose of [the impact investment] is to [accomplish a specific purpose]

---

[18] In some cases, the parties may agree that audits will only be necessary if requested by the investor and the cost of the audit may be allocated to the investor if a request is made more frequently than once every two or three unless the audit discloses substantial reporting errors.

[19] GIIRS uses the B-Lab's B Impact Assessment process to deliver a comprehensive accounting of a company's impact on workers, customers, communities, and the environment using IRIS metrics in conjunction with additional criteria. For further information, see https://b-analytics.net/giirs-funds. Measurement may also be conducted using other frameworks such as the IRIS, the Sustainable Accounting Standards Board Standards, Global Reporting Initiative Standards and the International Integrated Reporting Council framework.

[20] In addition to the contractual strategies outlined in the text, impact investors can require that enterprises operate as a benefit corporation (as discussed in the previous chapter) and/or that they specifically commit to pursuit of purposes aligned with universal standards such as the UN's Sustainable Development Goals.

for [a target population and geographical area], by [using a certain method]."[21]

- Obligation to respect a social business commitment in the company's charter document and/or bylaws using language such as the following: "The promoters shall respect a Social Business Charter, in the form attached hereto, which will provide that the managers of the Company will encourage social and environmental impacts, identify the indicators of such impact and prepare and distribute reports on such impact."

- Restriction on use of proceeds in accordance with a specific management plan that will lead to the accomplishment of the agreed social purpose using language such as the following: "The proceeds of the investment shall be used as operating capital in accordance with the management plans of the Company delivered to the Investor for implementation of the Company's products with mutually agreed upon partners, including development and testing of the Company's product and development of mobile features to make the product more accessible to low-income people."

- Awareness and endorsement of the social investment purpose using language such as the following: "The Company acknowledges that it is aware of and agrees with the Investor commitments in the area of ethics and sustainable development."

The Impact Terms Guide also described various incentives and disincentives that can be built into the terms of the deal and the investment agreements to ensure that the founders and other members of the management team are focused on pursuing and achieving the investor's social investment purposes. Examples included the following:

- Increase in founder/management equity stake relative to investor by providing for forfeiture of a portion of investor's

---

[21] A breach of the social investment purpose covenant should explicitly be called out as an event of default in the investment agreement that would trigger specific consequences detailed in the agreement.

equity if specific performance milestones are achieved using language such as the following: "[For every] OR [Upon completion of [specify impact target], the Company shall have the right to cause the forfeiture of up to [X Preferred Shares] or [X percent of the Preferred Shares], which forfeiture may be structured as a redemption of Preferred Shares at an agreed upon nominal value."

- Increase in founder/management equity stake relative to investor through alteration of redemption price to reflect the company's social or environmental performance using language such as the following: "[For every] OR [Upon completion of] [specify impact target], the redemption price per Share shall be reduced by X percent, provided that the price shall not be reduced below [$X per Share] OR [the Purchase Price] OR [a redemption price per Share equivalent to an X percent return per year on the Purchase Price]."

- Reduction in interest rate in debt transactions based on achievement of specific purposes using language such as the following: "[For every] OR [Upon completion of] [specify impact target], the rate of the Accruing Interest shall be reduced by X percent. In the aggregate, the interest due on the Maturity Date shall not be reduced by more than the total amount of the Accruing Interest."

- Increase in interest rate in debt transactions upon failure to achieve agreed performance metrics using language such as the following: "If during the term of the Loan the Company fails to cure the violation of [specify the penalty trigger] within X days, the interest rate shall be increased by X percent, provided that the interest rate shall not be increased above the Initial Rate plus X percent."

- Forced repurchase of investor's shares, through redemption, following a continuous failure of the company to achieve its specific purpose using language such as the following: "As long as any of the Preferred Shares remain outstanding, if [specify the redemption trigger], the Investor may require redemption of [all or any portion of the Preferred Shares held by the Investor] OR [all but not less than all of the Preferred Shares]."

Other approaches for embedding social mission and impact into deal structures and investment documentation mentioned by Burand included incorporating a social mission definition into the deal documentation; restricting the use of proceeds of the investment to financing those business operations that are driving social impact outcomes; establishing a governance structure for the investee that includes the appointment of a board member with the responsibility to oversee the investee's social impact; correlating financial returns to social impact outcomes actually achieved by the investee—either directly (i.e., the higher the social impact, the higher the expected financial return) or inversely (i.e., a lower financial return is required if a higher social impact return is achieved); and preserving the social mission objectives of investees, even at exit, through various techniques that have been referred to collectively as "mission lock".[22]

---

[22] Strategies used to establish and enforce "mission lock" include granting veto rights to the company's founders, who are presumably the parties most interested in maintaining control of the company's social mission, to block investor exits that conflict with the company's mission; termination of valuable licenses or hikes in the royalties/fees to be paid for such licenses; and the company's choice of legal form (e.g., benefit corporations, which are governed by guidance that allows directors to take into account all corporate constituencies, not just shareholders, when weighing offers to purchase the company, which means that a sale to the highest bidder is not mandated) and/or provisions relating to the purpose and authority of the entity included in the company's charter documents (e.g., provisions detailing specific socially-related public benefits and/or provisions that explicitly prohibit the company from taking certain actions in order to generate profits). Burand, D. 2015. "Resolving Impact Investment Disputes: When Doing Good Goes Bad." *Washington University Journal of Law & Policy* 48, no. 55, 65–67, https://openscholarship.wustl.edu/law_journal_law_policy/vol48/iss1/9

Mac Cormac et al. offered a menu of strategies that impact investors could draw upon to protect themselves against deviation from social mission by portfolio companies. For example, when the investment takes the form of convertible debt the following steps should be considered[23]:

- Require that the company's mission be memorialized at the time of the investment (e.g., in a new corporate form, corporate charter documents, shareholders' agreement, voting agreement, or in the debt instrument itself)
- Include affirmative covenants (e.g., borrower shall use the proceeds of an investment only in a mission-aligned fashion) or negative covenants (e.g., borrower shall not change its mission-aligned business plan; borrower shall not incur any material capital expenditures for activities that conflict with mission)
- Include material deviation from the company's defined mission as an event of default which triggers repayment of the outstanding debt, as opposed to a cross-default with other debt instruments that would have a catastrophic impact on an early-stage venture, and a supplemental remedy for investors in case the debt is not repaid, such as turning control of the board over to the investors
- Provide that a higher interest rate or prepayment will automatically apply if the borrower takes certain actions inconsistent with its mission
- Provide that equity conversion will not apply automatically in the next round of financing if the borrower takes certain actions inconsistent with the mission
- Require detailed reporting by the company to debtholders on mission and impact

---

[23] S. Mac Cormac, J. Finfrock and B. Fox, "Impact Investing" in A. Gutterman et al. (Editors), *The Lawyer's Corporate Social Responsibility Deskbook* (Chicago: American Bar Association, 2019), 234–235.

- Appoint a standing special committee of the board tasked with oversight of mission that reports to the board and the investors if there has been material deviation
- Establish the company's mission with reference to a third-party standard and provide for audits of the company's compliance with the standard by the third party on a regular basis

Mac Cormac et al. noted that it was important for the parties to include procedures for determining whether a "material deviation" from the company's defined mission had occurred, given the significant consequences of a default. One approach is for the investor to have the right to make an initial determination, but provide the company with an opportunity to object and have the dispute turned over to a designated independent third party to resolve. The third party audit referred to in the list is also a good way to reduce disputes.[24]

When the investment takes the form of preferred equity, Mac Cormac et al. advised impact investors to consider the following steps[25]:

- Enter into shareholder voting agreements that require that certain investors approve actions which are mission- (or not-mission-) aligned
- Create separate classes of stock for mission-aligned investors and founders, in conjunction with class approval rights for certain key actions such as material changes in the company's business plan, including changes to mission; a sale of the company, along with triggers for drag-along rights; or any action out of the ordinary course that could have a material impact on mission
- Guarantee board representation for mission-aligned investors or have an impact investor board designee have specific veto rights at the board level
- Include redemption rights in the event of a material deviation from mission which would require the company to repurchase

---

[24] Id. at 235.
[25] Id. at 235–236.

investors' shares or face specified penalties, such as ceding board control to the unredeemed investors until the redemption price is paid[26]

- Include information rights related to mission and impact reporting
- Provide for changes to the conversion formula or conversion ratio from preferred stock to common stock in the event of a material deviation from mission, which would result in the investors receiving more common shares upon conversion and increasing their ownership stake relative to the founders
- Specify that dividends to preferred shareholders will become cumulative (i.e., will have to be paid regardless of the company's profitability) in the event of material deviation from mission, which also increases the number of common shares received upon conversion and the liquidation preference of the preferred shares[27]
- Provide for changing the waterfall and/or the return upon liquidation (including a sale of the company) in the event of a deviation from mission[28]

---

[26] The risk that the company may be unable to fund a require repurchase may be managed by granting the investors the right to sell their shares to a co-investor who serves as a guarantor in the event of mission deviation.

[27] The number of common shares received upon conversion will increase because the amount of cumulative but unpaid dividends is added to the original amount paid by the investors for their shares. Similarly, the liquidation preference for the shares would be increased by the amount of cumulative but unpaid dividends.

[28] For example, provision could be made for changing the liquidation preference of the preferred shares from one time their original investment to a greater multiple, such as two times). Alternatively, or in addition, the preferred shares may be adjusted so that they become participating preferred rather than nonparticipating, which means that they would receive a greater share of the proceeds upon a sale of the company relative to the founders and other common shareholders. For further discussion, see A. Gutterman, *Launching New Businesses: A Guide for Sustainable Entrepreneurs* (Oakland CA: Sustainable Entrepreneurship Project, 2019) and C. Harvey, "Financing a Business" in A. Gutterman and R. Brown (Editors), *Emerging Companies Guide* (3rd Edition) (Chicago: American Bar Association Business Law Section, 2020), 213.

While impact investors should expect to make long-term commitments to their portfolio companies and hold their securities for a significant period of time, consideration needs to be given to exit strategies even before the deal is closed. One of the goals of impact investing is to create value for both the investors and the companies in which they invest, and value can only be measured and realized when the securities issued to the investors can be liquidated (e.g., sold in a public offering or sale of the company, redeemed by the company or, in the case of a debt instrument, retired by payment of outstanding principal and interest). The fund managers should press the managers of the company to create an exit plan based on realistic assumptions regarding the progress of the company toward its business, financial, and impact goals and the company's ability to raise additional capital to execute its strategies. It may be necessary, and expected, that the investor provide additional capital to the enterprise; however, as a general matter, the timeline of the investor's involvement with the company should extend no longer than the period during which the investor can make a significant contribution to the company's progress. The exit plan should, also address how the company's impact objectives will be maintained after the investors have exited and investors should be prepared to provide company managers with a reasonable amount of flexibility in terms of the timing of an exit transaction and the selection of a buyer in order to ensure that the impact-related activities of the company will be continued under reliable stewardship.[29]

Post-Investment Management

Impact investors choose and rely upon fund managers to not only make good choices about the selection of portfolio companies, but also to help and support the managers of those companies to achieve the mutually agreed financial and impact goals once the deal has closed. The terms of the investment should include commitments from both sides regarding post-investment management and communications and the fund

---

[29] See Schiff, H. and H. Dithrich. 2018. *Lasting Impact: The Need for Responsible Exits*, 20–23. New York, NY: The GIIN, January 2018, https://thegiin.org/research/publication/responsible-exits

managers should have a full team and formal structure in place to be sure that the fund can adequately support all of the companies that are included in the fund's portfolio. Each of the main fund managers will have a group of portfolio companies that he or she is primarily responsible for and the fund manager will need to have sufficient time to interact with the managers of those companies and oversee those members of the fund's operational team that have also been assigned to those companies. In addition, the fund managers must be prepared to leverage external resources and independent experts to support portfolio companies, such as by facilitating access for those companies to the networks of the fund's investors and providing those companies with introductions to outside parties that can offer technical and operational assistance to build their business capacities quickly and efficiently. Other suggestions from the GIIN for developing professional monitoring processes for portfolio companies include establishing annual portfolio monitoring cycle: quarterly review of investee reports and regular valuation; early identification of issues and problems: regular monitoring and early warning signs; taking early action to resolve issues and building capacity in portfolio monitoring teams to deal with issues when they arise; and offering optional common shared services for investees including finance, accounting, reporting, human resources and recruitment.[30]

The GIIN suggested that one area in which fund managers can provide useful and specific assistance to portfolio companies is with identifying specific risks confronting the companies in their operating environments and developing appropriate risk and crisis management programs. Specific risks depend on a variety of factors including the company's business model and the locations in which they are operating. Companies may find themselves challenged by natural disasters, societal upheavals, political tensions, labor disputes, and breaches of legal responsibilities. Fund managers need to work with the managers of their portfolio companies to create contingency plans and mitigate the loss of value to the fund's portfolio. Fund managers also need to be able to make specific

---

[30] https://thegiin.org/developing-a-private-equity-fund-foundation-and-structure/

contributions to the responses of portfolio companies to a crisis, either directly or through their networks. [31]

Fund managers often provide proactive support for their portfolio companies by serving as members of their board of directors. In their role as a director, the fund manager can take a number of steps to strengthen the company's governance framework and processes including requesting an evaluation of the company's governance to achieve best practice; reviewing or establishing a code of ethics, veto and other rights; defining the company's charter and decision-making processes; clarifying the role of the board of directors in the form of a charter; and ensuring that all directors and officers understand their duties and responsibilities to the company and its stakeholders. Even though the portfolio company may still be relatively small, the closing of an investment by an impact fund should be a point of transition toward a more focused approach to governance that includes the formation of specialized board committees addressing issues such as audits, compensation and remuneration, governance, and organizational development.[32]

Regardless of whether a fund has a representative on the board of directors, the fund managers and their team members should commit to continuous support of the management team leveraging the fund managers' experience and strong knowledge about the industry and sector in which the company is operating and the technology and operational strategies upon which the success of the company depends. The GIIN noted that fund managers can provide their portfolio companies with guidance by[33]:

- Advising on the company's business strategy, including product design and marketing
- Using gap analysis to uncover new functional needs for a growth company
- Helping to attract and retain quality senior staff

---

[31] https://thegiin.org/developing-a-private-equity-fund-foundation-and-structure/ (Figure 15: Crisis Management)

[32] Id.

[33] Id.

- Improving financial systems, including accounting, audit, and reporting procedures
- Introducing the company to other sources of financing
- Improving its governance and transparency[34]
- Introducing the company to new technology
- Establishing new supply and distribution relationships
- Helping the company effectively measure and manage for impact
- Helping the company to use social and environmental impact data to strengthen sales and impact performance
- Identifying and planning for exit options

Guidance opportunities and priorities can also be broken out into functional categories: strategy (help define growth strategy and business plan and develop impact measurement and management plan); human resources (bring in CFO or financial manager, if needed, and surface the best talent available within budget); governance (strengthen governance at the board level and identify board members who are aligned with the company's environmental and social mission); operations (improve and develop products, identify improved production methods and review relationships with suppliers); and finance (review financing structure and identify areas of improvement, help identify sources of capital, and introduce information management systems and budgeting processes).[35]

---

[34] Fund managers can provide advice on governance issues related to environmental and social issues, even if not directly related to the specific impact objective of the investment. See, for example, *How to Set Up Effective Climate Governance on Corporate Boards: Guiding Principles and Questions* (World Economic Forum, January 2019), http://www3.weforum.org/docs/WEF_Creating_effective_climate_governance_on_corporate_boards.pdf

[35] https://thegiin.org/developing-a-private-equity-fund-foundation-and-structure/ (Figure 16: Adding Value Across the Investment Lifecycle and Figure 17: Adding Value: Function Model)

CHAPTER 6

Impact Measurement and Reporting

Impact investing requires an intention to generate social and environmental impact alongside a financial return, which means that impact investors must have a means for identify and measuring "impact" and reporting on the results of their efforts to the ultimate owners of the assets that are being invested. One of the challenges with the evolution of impact investing has been developing reliable and consistent measures and ratings of performance (i.e., environmental and/or social impact) for individual projects and the overall progress of enterprises with respect to environmental, social, and governance (ESG) criteria. A number of ESG ratings schemes have emerged and companies have been provided with opportunities to seek and obtain certification of their sustainability credentials by external assessors. As time has gone by there has been more interest in quantifying the relative environmental and social impacts of projects and companies in order to facilitate comparisons and there is also greater scrutiny of the ESG ratings schemes themselves. However, many have pointed to the difficulties of gauging social impact as opposed to environmental matters. For example, while reductions in pollution can be measured, the relative value of supporting and enabling ongoing education of young people in a developing country cannot be distilled down into a number and each investor will need to assess such a project by reference to his or her own ethical lens and personal value system.[1]

In order to measure performance, impact investors and the enterprises in which they invest must be able to collect and analyze appropriate data. Godeke and Briaud observed that the availability of ESG data and

---

[1] "The Economist Explains: What is Sustainable Finance?" The Economist, April 17, 2018. https://economist.com/the-economist-explains/2018/04/17/what-is-sustainable-finance

data providers has proliferated, but that consistency does not yet exist across approaches. A range of ESG data services are available including fundamental providers of public data (e.g., Bloomberg and Refinitiv), comprehensive ESG ratings providers (e.g., ISS, MSCI, RepRisk, Sustainalytics, and Vigeo Eiris) and specialists that focus their work on specific themes (e.g., the nonprofit Carbon Disclosure Project and Equileap (gender-equality data)). Data providers must gather and assess an exploding universe of data that is no longer limited to corporate disclosures but now extends to information from nongovernmental organizations, governments, and other stakeholders tracking various aspects of the ESG practices of companies. In order to keep up, data providers have deployed new technologies—machine learning, natural language processing, and artificial intelligence—to identify and interpret patterns and signals in the data.[2]

According to So and Capanyola, the measurement methods used by impact investors can be grouped into four main categories[3]:

- *Expected return methods,* **which** weigh the anticipated benefits of an investment against its costs (e.g., the social return on investment (SROI) method, which is discussed below and focuses on calculating an investment's present social value of impact compared to the value of the inputs).
- *Theory of change methods,* **which** outline the intended process for achieving social impact using a logic model that maps the linkages between input, activities, output, outcomes, and impact and also takes into consideration impact risks

[2] Godeke, S., and P. Briaud. 2020. *Impact Investing Handbook: An Implementation Guide for Practitioners*, 96. Rockefeller Philanthropy Advisors. (see Exhibit 4–7 for information on the evolution of ESG research from scarcity (i.e., What can I discover about the ESG record of a company?) to abundance (i.e., What does all the data mean? How do I differentiate companies?) to superabundance (i.e., How do I find ESG signals in unstructured data?)).

[3] So, I., and A. Capanyola. 2016. "How Impact Investors Actually Measure Impact." *Stanford Social Innovation Review*, May 16, 2016, https://ssir.org/articles/entry/how_impact_investors_actually_measure_impact

(i.e., the factors that could jeopardize achievement of the expected impact).

- *Mission alignment methods,* **which** measure the execution of strategy against the project's mission and end goals over time using scorecards or social value criteria to monitor and manage key performance metrics relating to operational performance, organizational effectiveness, finances, and social value.
- *Experimental and quasi-experimental methods,* **which** include "after-the-fact" evaluations using randomized control trials or other counterfactual approaches to determine the impact of an intervention compared to the situation if the intervention had not taken place.

So and Capanyola observed that impact investors use impact measurements for different purposes during different parts of the investment cycle that they broke out into the following phases: first, estimating impact while conducting due diligence to assess the potential social return before committing to an investment; second, planning impact by choosing the metrics and data collection methods that the investor will use to monitor a program's effects; third, monitoring impact after the investment has been made and throughout the life of the investment through measuring and analysis of data to track the intervention's efforts; and finally, evaluating impact by measuring an investment's social consequences after the program concludes to assess portfolio performance and next steps for the investor, including re-investment.[4] Impact measurement has long been perceived as challenging given the slow evolution of global standards and many investors have attempted to avoid the costly steps required to accurately gauge the social impact of their investments. As a result, impact investors often focus on outputs, meaning the activities produced by the investment, instead of outcomes, and on the actual social impact created by the investment; base confidence on intuition and judgment rather than hard metrics; and use point in time metrics which consider the impact at one-time period versus over a full investment lifecycle.[5]

---

[4] Id.

[5] Malik, Z. 2019. "The How-To: Measuring Outcomes Of Impact Investing." May 15, 2019, https://entrepreneur.com/article/333650

Parameters of Impact

Brest and Born described an impact investor as someone seeking to produce beneficial social or environmental outcomes that would not occur but for his or her investment in a social enterprise, a concept often referred to as "additionality," and defined the practice of "impact investing" as "actively placing capital in enterprises that generate social or environmental goods, services, or ancillary benefits (such as creating jobs), with expected financial returns ranging from the highly concessionary to above market."[6] They went on to explore three parameters of impact: the impact of the enterprise itself, which means the social outcomes it produces that would not otherwise have occurred; investors' contribution to the enterprise's impact; and the contribution of non-monetary activities to the enterprise's impact. They noted that in order for an investment or non-monetary activities to have impact it must increase the quantity or quality of the enterprise's social outcomes beyond what would otherwise have occurred.

Brest and Born explained that enterprises could have impact in several possible ways, beginning with "product impact," which is the impact of the goods or service produced by the enterprise (e.g., providing clean water, financial services, or efficient energy), and "operational impact," which is the impact of the enterprise's management practices on its employees' health and economic security, its effect on jobs or other aspects of the well-being of the community in which it operates, or the environmental effects of its supply chain and operations.[7] Brest and Born pointed out that an enterprise's product or operational impact can be multiplied if and when the enterprise collaborates with others, such as when businesses, government agencies, nonprofits, and foundations act together to address a particular environmental or social issue. Products and services of enterprises may also have an impact beyond its own goals and mission in the markets and sectors in which they are operating (e.g., development

---

[6] Brest, P., and K. Born. 2013. "Unpacking the Impact in Impact Investing." *Stanford Social Innovation Review*, August 14, 2013. (citing "Investing for Impact" (Bridges Ventures and Parthenon Group), 3). When they used the term "social outcomes", Brest and Born were referring to both environmental and social objectives.

[7] Id. (citing Olsen, S., and B. Galimidi. 2012. "Catalog of Approaches to Impact Measurement." *Social Venture Technology Group*, July 10, 2012).

of supply chains and positive spillover effects for other businesses in the community in which the enterprise is operating). As for identifying and measuring impact, Brest and Born pointed out that investors need to consider both "outputs," which is a measure of the beneficial product or operational impact (e.g., the number of units of a product manufactured and distributed to a target population), and "outcomes," which is a measure of the actual effect of the outputs on improving people's lives and positively addressing the particular social issue.[8]

As far as an investor's contribution to the enterprise's impact, Brest and Born argued that the test should be grounded in "additionality" and focus on whether the investment increased the quantity or quality of the enterprise's social output beyond what would otherwise have occurred. Assuming that the enterprise has the capacity to absorb more capital, an investment has impact if it provides more capital, or capital at lower cost, to the enterprise than would have been the case if the investment had not been made. Situations in which impact investors can provide benefits to enterprises from the form and terms of their investment include below market ("concessionary") investments, loan guarantees, subordinated debt or equity positions, longer terms before exit, and flexibility in adapting the terms of investments to the enterprise's needs and business model.

With regard to impactful non-monetary activities, Brest and Born noted that fund managers, investors and other actors could improve the social outputs of enterprises by providing one or more of the following benefits:

- Improving the enabling social, political, and regulatory environment for social enterprises and investors by developing scoring and rating models and improving the rule of law

---

[8] Brest and Born used the example of a situation where an enterprise was manufacturing and distributing bed nets with the goal of reducing morbidity and mortality from malaria and explained that the "output" was the quantity and quality of the enterprise's manufacturing and distribution activities (e.g., how many were actually distributed and did they perform in accordance with specifications) and "outcome" was the degree to which the bed nets actually reduced malaria in the target population, a challenging question because it is often difficult to isolate and measure the specific contribution that the bed nets may have made to any reduction.

- Impact investment intermediaries supporting identification and promotion of impact investment opportunities
- Aggregating capital and providing other investment services, such as technical assistance to investors, to reduce transaction costs by creating economies of scale
- Providing technical and governance assistance to enterprises, including market information, and helping them build strategic relationships with customers, suppliers, and other partners
- Gaining socially neutral investors (i.e., investors who demand market returns) in order to expand the pool of available capital for enterprises, which can occur when a respected early-round investor signals that initial goals have been achieved and that follow-on investment warrant consideration
- Securing and protecting the enterprise's social mission by embedding the mission deeply into the enterprise through contractual arrangements, benefit corporation status and other types of venture structuring or "B Corporation" certification

Impact Measurement and Management

Impact measurement and management (IMM) has been described as the process by which impact investors can understand the effects of their investments on people and the planet (i.e., measurement) and then determine the appropriate actions to take to adapt the processes that are being used and improve their outcomes (i.e., management). IMM is an evolving field, still significantly young in relation to the theories and frameworks that have been developed for measuring financing performance. IMM includes a number of different tools including monitoring and evaluation, ratings, key performance indicators and disclosures, and research continues toward development of best practices. IMM can and should be used by impact investors for several important purposes including understanding whether the short-term changes and long-term effects from an investment are playing out as anticipated, identifying methods and opportunities for improving the impact performance of an investment and building a knowledge base that can be used for making better decisions about future investments.[9]

Impact investors can choose from among various principles, frameworks, and standards when developing strategies for measuring and managing the impact of their investments. Principles include rules and best practices to ensure the overall integrity of processes and behaviors and examples include the IFC Operating Principles for Impact Management, the Principles for Responsible Investment, and the Impact Management Principles of the European Venture Philanthropy Association. Principles are not specific measurement techniques; their purpose is to communicate the intentions of the investor with respect to engaging in IMM.[10] For example, the IFC Operating Principles for Impact Management were launched at the World Bank Group/IMF Spring Meetings in 2019 and include the following steps through each of the typical stages of investment (i.e., strategic intent, origination and structuring, portfolio management and impact at exit)[11]:

1. Define strategic impact objective(s) consistent with the investment strategy
2. Manage strategic impact and financial returns at portfolio level
3. Establish the investor's contribution to the achievement of impact
4. Assess the expected impact of each investment, based on a systematic approach
5. Assess, address, monitor and manage the potential risks of negative effects of each investment
6. Monitor the progress of each investment in achieving impact against expectations and respond appropriately
7. Conduct exits, considering the effect on sustained impact
8. Review, document, and improve decisions and processes based on the achievement of impact and lessons learned

---

[9] Godeke, S. and P. Briaud. 2020. *Impact Investing Handbook: An Implementation Guide for Practitioners*, 122. Rockefeller Philanthropy Advisors.

[10] Id. at 126.

[11] https://impactprinciples.org/principles

9. Publicly disclose alignment with the principles and provide independent verification of the extent of alignment

Frameworks are used to implement the intentions of the impact investor expressed in the principles referred to above and include specific methodologies for organizing IMM such as the United Nation's Sustainable Development Goals (SDGs), the G8 Impact Measurement Working Group Report and Acumen, through its Lean Data Project.[12] The IMM program structure recommended by the G8 Impact Measurement Working Group includes the following four phases[13]:

- "Plan" including articulating the desired impact of investments by selecting goals and outcomes and determining the metrics to be used for assessing the performance of investments
- "Do" including capturing and storing data in a timely and organized fashion and validating the date to ensure that is of sufficient quality
- "Assess" by analyzing the collected and verified data to distill insights
- "Review" including sharing progress with key stakeholders through reporting and identifying and implementing mechanisms to strengthen the rigor of the investment process and outcomes

An example of how a framework might be used is provided by the Impact Management Project (IMP), which has created a community of over 2,000 enterprises, investors, and practitioners to build a global consensus on how to talk about, measure, and manage ESG risks and positive impacts.[14] The IMP defines impact as a change in an outcome

---

[12] Godeke, S. and P. Briaud. 2020. *Impact Investing Handbook: An Implementation Guide for Practitioners*, 126. Rockefeller Philanthropy Advisors.

[13] Id. at 131.

[14] The discussion in this section of the Impact Management Project and its dimensions for measuring impact performance is based on https://impactmanagementproject.com/impact-management/impact-management-norms/

caused by an organization, noting that impacts can be positive or negative and intended or unintended. Based on its consultations, the IMP concluded that impact can be deconstructed and measured across five dimensions: What, Who, How Much, Contribution, and Risk. Each of these dimensions includes the following:

- "What" tells us what outcome the enterprise is contributing to during the measurement period, whether it is positive or negative and how important the outcome is to the stakeholders who are experiencing it.
- "Who" tells us which stakeholders are experiencing the outcome and how underserved they are in relation to the outcome.
- "How Much" tells us how many stakeholders experienced the outcome, what degree of change they experienced and how long they experienced the outcome.
- "Contribution" tells us whether an enterprise's and/or investor's efforts resulted in outcomes that were likely better than what would have occurred otherwise; in other words, would the change likely have happened anyway.
- "Risk" tells us the likelihood that impact will be different than expected and also considers the risk to people and plant that impact does not occur as expected.

The IMP has developed a set of 15 impact data categories that provide information across the five dimensions that can be used by enterprises and investors to set goals and assess impact performance. For example, there are four impact data categories for the "What" impact dimension:

- Outcome level in period: The level of outcome (positive or negative, intended, or unintended) experienced by the stakeholder when engaging with the enterprise
- Outcome threshold: The level of outcome that the stakeholder considers to be a positive outcome, with anything below this level being considered a negative outcome

- Importance of outcome to stakeholder: The stakeholder's view, ideally expressed by them directly, of whether the outcome they experience is important (relevant to other outcomes)
- SDG or other global goal: The SDG or other global sustainability goal that outcome relates to

Data categories for the other dimensions include stakeholder, geographical boundary, outcome level at baseline, and stakeholder characteristics for "Who"; scale, depth, and duration for "How Much"; depth and duration counterfactual for "Contribution," and risk types and levels for "Risk." Understanding the required data categories allows impact investors to develop appropriate data collection and reporting requirements for each of their investments and incorporate them into the investment documentation and their relationships with the managers of the enterprises in which they invest.

Gauging and projecting impact of an investment before it is made is understandably difficult; however, it is obviously an essential part of the due diligence process for any new impact investment. Godeke and Briaud explained that there are a number of different approaches to impact due diligence and that best practices would be to rely on a combination of qualitative and quantitative approaches. For example, the process can begin with an impact-focused due diligence questionnaire based on a standard list of questions that will often be customized to the specific investee and the anticipated form of impact. The goal of the questionnaire is to identify linkages with the components of the theory of change and identify areas of potential misalignment. Investors can also use quantitative impact due diligence tools based on weighted criteria. Qualitative information should be collected through "storytelling" that helps the investor understand how change is occurring.[15]

Data categories for assessing outcomes have been listed above, but it is not always easy to gather qualitative information from the projected beneficiaries of an impact intervention. The IMP has suggested the use of two types of self-reported data (i.e., data collected from surveys of actual

---

[15] Godeke, S. and P. Briaud. 2020. *Impact Investing Handbook: An Implementation Guide for Practitioners*, 132. Rockefeller Philanthropy Advisors.

beneficiaries): subjective self-reported data (e.g., "I know more than I did before the course" or "I feel better this year compared to last year") and objective self-reported data (e.g., "I was offered a job shortly after completing the course" or "I went to a doctor three times of the last year compared to 15 times the year before"). The narrative statements from beneficiaries can be supplemented by collecting relevant objective data such as evidence relating to their completion and passage of a course with a specified minimum score and changes in measures of physical health such as blood pressure levels.[16]

Standards include taxonomies and core metrics that are applied to specific industries, sectors and themes in order to measure progress toward impact goals. Examples of standards include the standards developed by the Sustainability Accounting Standards Board and B Lab, as well as the Global Impact Investing Rating System (GIIRS) and the Impact Reporting and Investment Standards (IRIS+) launched by the GIIN as a freely available catalog of generally accepted performance metrics that impact investors can use to measure, manage, and optimize their impact.[17] The latest IRIS framework references the IMP's five dimensions of impact and the SDGs and includes metrics for the following categories[18]:

- Financial performance, including standard financial reporting metrics such as current assets and financial liabilities
- Operational performance, including parameters to assess investees' governance policies, employment practices, and the social and environmental impact of their day-to-day business activities
- Product performance, including metrics that describe and quantify the social and environmental benefits of the products, services, and unique processes offered by target companies
- Sector performance, including metrics that define and quantify impact in particular social and environmental sectors, including agriculture, financial services, and health care

---

[16] Id. at 136.

[17] Id. at 129. A comprehensive list of standards is available at https://iris.thegiin.org/aligned-standards/

[18] https://impactterms.org/impact-terms-guide/

- Social and environmental objective performance, including metrics that describe and quantify progress toward specific impact objectives such as employment generation or sustainable land use

One of the key features of IRIS+ is that it is a thematic taxonomy based on generally accepted Impact Categories and Impact Themes which identifies common goals and core metrics sets by theme, thereby providing a shared language for describing, assessing, communicating, and ultimately comparing impact performance. IRIS+ is organized according to the social and environmental Impact Themes by which impact investors (and the enterprises or projects in which they invest) frame their strategic goals, portfolios, and business models including agriculture, air, biodiversity and ecosystems, climate, diversity and inclusion, education, employment, energy, financial services, health, land, oceans and coastal zones, pollution, real estate, waste, and water. Each theme includes a described of associated strategic goals and delivery models. For example, themes in real estate include strategic goals and delivery models that seek to provide housing projects, services, and infrastructure for which the associated financial costs to occupants do not threaten or compromise their enjoyment of other human rights and basic needs and represent a reasonable proportion of occupants' individual overall incomes. Subthemes within real estate include affordable quality housing, which is focused on social impact, and green buildings, which is focused on environmental impact. Strategic goals for affordable housing include improving housing quality, increasing residential stability, increasing housing affordability, and increasing access to supportive services through housing. Delivery models for affordable housing include housing acquisition, development, and preservation (both rental and ownership, includes mortgages); housing management (service providers) and supportive housing services (including employment, physical and mental health services, rental subsidies, and links to public transport). Housing financing, which would be measured by metrics such as the number of housing units financed and the number of individuals housed, is addressed in the financial services theme.[19]

---

[19] IRIS+ Thematic Taxonomy (Global Impact Investing Network, May 2019). With respect to measurement of the impact of projects related to financing

Social Return on Investment

A commonly used tool for impact evaluation is Social Return on Investment (SROI), which has been described as a systematic way of incorporating social, environmental, economic, and other values into decision-making processes that creates a holistic perspective on whether a development project or social business or enterprise is beneficial and profitable.[20] As is the case with traditional cost–benefit analysis, SROI includes a ratio, referred to as a SROI ratio; however, the SROI ratio is not used as a means for comparing various projects but rather as an aid in developing the narrative for a particular project. Advocates of the SROI approach have stressed that stakeholder perspectives are essential and the goal of the SROI process, which involves extensive consultation with stakeholders (particularly the key beneficiaries of the project), is to assess the value of the project from the stakeholders' perspectives.

The steps of the SROI process include defining the scope and boundaries (objectives and scope) of the project and analysis (i.e., issues to be addressed and the objectives in addressing them); identification and selection of key stakeholders, particularly those stakeholders who will be most impacted by the project; engagement of stakeholders to identify their perceptions of important outcomes and develop the theory of change or business plan for the project which is based on mapping the relationships among the organization's resources and activities and the outcomes for each stakeholder; identifying "what goes in" (i.e., inputs for each outcome) and "what comes out" (i.e., results) for each intended outcome; development of indicators for measuring inputs, activities, and outcomes, with a particular emphasis on outcomes; quantifying the impact of the organization's efforts, translating the articulated benefits and costs into a monetary value and calculating the SROI ratio by comparing the investments (inputs) on the one hand and the financial, social,

---

affordable housing units, see Evaluating Impact Performance: Housing Investments (Global Impact Investing Network, 2019).

[20] The discussion of SROI in this paragraph is adapted from "What is the relationship between IRIS and SROI?" by Social Value UK and M. Salverda, Social Return on Investment, (BetterEvaluation), http://betterevaluation.org/approach/SROI

and environmental returns (outcomes and impact of an intervention) on the other. The SROI should be placed in context with narratives that provide context for the numbers and explain what cannot be captured in the SROI ratio alone. The entire process should be continuously verified and the end product should be a SROI report that communicates the results to all stakeholders, explains the steps that were taken and serves as a foundation for future steps including adjustments to the business plan. While the SROI methods provides a process that can be followed in order to determine what impact indicators to measure, the output will only be credible if there is a good and consistent understanding of how each of those indicators will be measured, a challenge that can be addressed by reliance on the IRIS+ standards described above.

External Reviews

While impact investors can select their own tools for measuring the impact of their investments and require their investees to implement performance measurement and assessment systems, planning for external reviews of impact performance by independent expert organizations is a reasonable and prudent check on the actions and decisions of the managers of the enterprise. In its Green Bond Principles (GBP) and Social Bond Principles (SBP), the International Capital Market Association suggested four different types of independent external reviews that issuers could use to assess and demonstrate the alignment of their Green/Social Bonds or bond program to the core components that are included in both the GBP and SBP[21]:

- *Second Party Opinion:* An institution with environmental expertise, that is independent from the issuer and its adviser for its Green/Social Bond framework, can issue a second party opinion following an assessment of the issuer's overar-

---

[21] *Green Bond Principles: Voluntary Process Guidelines for Issuing Green Bonds* (Paris: International Capital Market Association, June 2018) and *Social Bond Principles: Voluntary Process Guidelines for Issuing Social Bonds* (Paris: International Capital Market Association, June 2020).

ching objectives, strategy, policy, and/or processes relating to environmental and/or social sustainability and an evaluation of the environmental and/or social features of the type of projects intended for the use of proceeds.

- *Verification:* Issuers can obtain independent verification of their Green/Social Bonds against a designated set of criteria typically related to business processes and/or environmental/social criteria. The GBP/SBP noted various types of verification including evaluation of the environmentally sustainable features of underlying assets and assurance or attestation regarding an issuer's internal tracking method for use of proceeds, allocation of funds from Green/Social Bond proceeds, statement of environmental/social impact or alignment of reporting with the GBP/SBP.

- *Certification:* Issuers can have their Green/Social Bond or associated Green/Social Bond framework or use of proceeds certified against a recognized external green or social standard or label which defines specific criteria and then requires testing for alignment with such criteria by qualified, accredited third parties.

- *Green/Social Bond Scoring/Rating:* Issuers can have their Green/Social Bond, associated Green/Social Bond framework or a key feature thereof such as use of proceeds evaluated or assessed by qualified third parties, such as specialized research providers or rating agencies, according to an established scoring/rating methodology that focuses on, among other things, environmental/social performance data or the process relative to the GBP/SBP.[22]

One important and widely used tool for independent impact certification and rating is the Global Impact Investing Ratings System (GIIRS) has been described as a comprehensive, comparable, and transparent

---

[22] The GBP/SBP noted that Green/Social Bond Scoring/Rating is different from credit ratings, but pointed out that credit ratings also reflect material environmental/social risks.

system for assessing the social and environmental impact of companies and funds with a ratings and analytics approach analogous to Morningstar Investment rankings.[23] Another valuable aspect of GIIRS is its collection of aggregated impact data and ratings information in a product called GIIRS Ratings & Analytics that organizations can use when assessing and reporting social and environmental impact. GIIRS, which is powered by B Analytics (https://b-analytics.net/), provides a composite score by assessing performance in several impact categories including workers, customers, communities, and the environment, each of which are weighted in advance based on geography, sector, and size. The ratings process begins with completion of an online GIIRS Assessment, which is based on the B Impact Assessment used to certify "B corporations," and continues with an assessment review by GIIRS staff that includes interviews and a desk review of selected documents provided by the enterprise at the request of GIIRS.

Reporting

In order to know whether or not an enterprise is achieving its goals relating to impact performance it is necessary to have in place procedures for reporting and otherwise communicating information regarding impact performance to the enterprise's stakeholders. While certain corporate sustainability disclosures have now become minimum legal requirements in some jurisdictions, in general such disclosures are still a voluntary matter and directors have some leeway as to the scope of the disclosure made by their companies and how they are presented to investors and other stakeholders. Some companies continue to limit their disclosures to those are specifically required by regulators; however, most companies have realized that they need to pay attention to the issues raised by institutional investors and other key stakeholders and make sure that they are covered in the disclosure program. At the other extreme, there are companies that have embraced sustainability as integral to their brands and have elected to demonstrate their commitment by preparing and disseminating

---

[23] GIIRS and SROI: What is the relationship?, Social Value UK.

additional disclosures that illustrate how they have woven sustainability into their long-term strategies and day-to-day operational activities.[24]

The scope of the company's reporting and verification efforts will depend on various factors including the size of the company, the stage of development and focus of its impact commitments, legal requirements, the financial and human resources available for investment in those activities, and the degree to which companies want and are able to integrate sustainability indicators into their traditional reporting of financial results. The Coalition for Environmentally Responsible Economics (Ceres), a nonprofit organization advocating for sustainability leadership (www.ceres.org), has developed and disseminated its Ceres Roadmap as a resource to help companies reengineer themselves to confront and overcome environmental and social challenges and as a guide toward corporate sustainability leadership.[25] In the area of disclosure and reporting, Ceres stated that the overall vision was that companies would report regularly on their sustainability strategy and performance, and that disclosure would include credible, standardized, independently verified metrics encompassing all material stakeholder concerns, and details of goals and plans for future action. Specific expectations regarding disclosure were as follows:

- D1—Standards for Disclosure: Companies will disclose all relevant sustainability information using the Global Reporting Initiative Guidelines as well as additional sector-relevant indicators.
- D2—Disclosure in Financial Filings: Companies will disclose material sustainability risks and opportunities, as well as performance data, in financial filings.
- D3—Scope and Content: Companies will regularly disclose trended performance data and targets relating to global direct operations, subsidiaries, joint ventures, products, and supply

---

[24] For further discussion of Sustainability Reporting, see Gutterman, A. 2020. *Sustainability Reporting and Communications.* New York, NY: Business Experts Press.
[25] Ceres, The Ceres Roadmap for Sustainability (www.ceres.org/ceresroadmap)

chains. Companies will demonstrate integration of sustainability into business systems and decision making, and disclosure will be balanced, covering challenges as well as positive impacts.

- D4—Vehicles for Disclosure: Companies will release sustainability information through a range of disclosure vehicles including sustainability reports, annual reports, financial filings, corporate websites, investor communications, and social media.
- D5—Verification and Assurance: Companies will verify key sustainability performance data to ensure valid results and will have their disclosures reviewed by an independent, credible third party.

In order to assure the quality of sustainability reporting and facilitate the efficient creation of comparable reports, it is necessary to have robust reporting standards that can be applied in a global economy in which the operational activities and reporting responsibilities of companies transcend national borders. International organizations, such as the United Nations (UN); regional organizations, such as the European Union (EU), and stock exchanges and independent organizations, such as the Global Reporting Initiative (GRI), have all been involved in the development and implementation of key international initiatives on sustainability reporting. Many of these initiatives take the form of national policies and instruments that incorporate elements of international or corporate social responsibility reporting frameworks. For example, The GRI Standards are referenced in government or market instruments in dozens of countries around the world, such as the preamble of the EU Directive on disclosure of non-financial and diversity information, and are frequently one of several normative or management standards referred to in reporting instruments, usually accompanied by references to the UN Global Compact, OECD Guidelines for Multinational Enterprises, and the ISO 26000 Guidance Standard on Social Responsibility.[26]

---

[26] Carrots & Sticks: Global Trends in Sustainability Reporting Regulation and Policy (KPMG International, the Global Research Initiative ("GRI"), the United Nations Environment Programme ("UNEP") and the Centre for Corporate Governance in Africa, 2016), available at www.carrotsandsticks.net, 23.

Mandatory reporting of ESG remains the exception rather than the rule in most jurisdictions, although the EU has adopted a directive on non-financial reporting that requires larger companies to report on ESG issues.[27] The Swiss Finance Institute (SFI) highlighted several of the challenges relating to measurement, quantification and reporting of ESG issues including the inherent difficulty in quantifying and aggregating complex, often qualitative, environmental and social issues, causes, costs, and impacts and the lack of universal legal obligations to report using a comprehensive, unified, and standardized reporting framework.[28] On the second point, the SFI noted that while a directive had been approved by the EC for implementation throughout the EU, each country would have their own country-specific laws that may differ substantially from one another and thus result in reporting that is less standardized than traditional financial reporting. The SFI pointed out that several voluntary sustainability reporting frameworks had been developed, including the GRI and the Sustainability Accounting Standards Board for companies and the UN Principles of Responsible Investing for investors; however, the SFI criticized the quality of the available non-financial information (research has found that ESG measurements from different data providers are often inconsistent) and argued that attempts to product credit rating-like ESG measurements were flawed because such measurements were not necessarily public information and changes in methods or ratings were typically not announced publicly.[29]

---

[27] Krauss, A., P. Kruger and J. Meyer. 2016. *Sustainable Finance in Switzerland: Where Do We Stand?*, 17. Zurich: Swiss Finance Institute. The SFI also noted that the stock exchanges in Johannesburg and London required disclosures on carbon emissions and other ESG issues and that countries such as France had adopted disclosure requirements for institutional investors. Id.

[28] Id. (citing Rowley, T., and S. Berman. 2000. "A Brand New Brand of Social Performance." *Business and Society* 38, p. 109; and *Policy Briefing: Financial Stability and Environmental Stability*. Cambridge Institute for Sustainability Leadership and United Nations Environment Programme, September 2015. (noting that environmental issues are difficult to quantify due to their interconnectedness and the uncertainty relating to when, how often, and how strongly environmental risks materialize)).

[29] Id. at 18.

In a report issued on July 6, 2020, the US Government Accountability Office evaluated the state of public company disclosures related to ESG issues and found, among other things, that it can be expected that investors will continue to pressure public companies to provide more detailed disclosure about their ESG initiatives and results of those initiatives to enable investors to track and eventually compare performance and that investors were concerned with "gaps and inconsistencies in companies' disclosures that limit their usefulness" and comparability.[30] For example, there was no consistency among the companies regarding the metrics that they used to report on the same topics and companies often changed the metrics they used to report on a topic from year-to-year, making it difficult to make comparisons over time and across companies. In addition, companies often failed to fully disclose the results of their activities relating to management of ESG-related risks or opportunities. Another problem for investors in easily finding all of the ESG-related disclosures of a company in one place, since most companies distribute such information in a variety of different ways including annual reports, proxy statements, multi-issue sustainability reports, single-issue reports, dynamic webpages, investor presentations, earnings calls, and shareholder bulletins. The report also found that investors have identified and affirmed linkages between positive ESG activity and financial value and, as such, have increasingly incorporated ESG performance into their voting decisions at annual meetings of the public companies in which they have invested.

---

[30] Public Companies: Disclosure of Environmental, Social and Governance Factors and Options to Enhance Them (US Government Accountability Office, GAO-20-530, July 2020). It was reported that the US Government Accountability Office ("GAO") analyzed the disclosures of 32 large and midsize public companies on 33 topics related to climate change, resource management, human rights, personnel management, workforce diversity, occupational health and safety, board accountability, and data security; and interviewed 14 large and midsize institutional investors (seven private-sector asset management firms and seven public pension funds), 18 public companies, 13 market observers (including nongovernmental ESG standard-setting organizations, academics, and other groups), and stock exchange and industry association representatives. H. Gregory, H. Palmer, and L. Wood, Emerging Trends in ESG Disclosures Highlighted in U.S. GAO Report (August 1, 2020).

While regulators such as the Securities and Exchange Commission are cognizant and attentive to changes in expected ESG disclosures, for the timing being leadership will continue to come from nongovernmental standard setters and framework developers such as the GRI and SASB.[31]

There are a variety of frameworks and tools that organizations can leverage in order to develop their sustainability strategies and reporting processes. Many of these take a comprehensive approach and have achieved international recognition. In addition, companies can turn to standards that are focused on single issues such as greenhouse gas emissions, climate change, or the impacts of business activity on forests.[32] It has been noted that distinctions can be made among normative, management and reporting frameworks with respect to sustainability strategies and reporting. For example, the UN Global Compact principles and the OECD Guidelines provide normative frameworks to help companies shape their sustainability vision and management approach, as well as to measure their impacts. ISO 26000 is an example of a management standard that organizations can use with respect to their corporate social responsibility strategies, processes, and activities. The reporting perspective is represented by the GRI's Sustainability Reporting Standards, which provide organizations with disclosure items and metrics that align with the most important international normative frameworks. Adding to the complexity is the emergence of sector-specific performance measurement and reporting frameworks, such as the GRESB for assessing ESG performance in the global commercial real estate sector. In addition, companies operating in specific sectors must take into account recommendations of sectoral trade associations, such as the guidance on reporting and communications discussed elsewhere in this publication provided by Finnish Textile & Fashion, the central organization for textile, clothing, and fashion companies in Finland.[33]

---

[31] Id.

[32] Krauss, A., P. Kruger and J. Meyer. 2016. *Sustainable Finance in Switzerland: Where Do We Stand?*, 25. Zurich: Swiss Finance Institute.

[33] 2016. *Finnish Textile & Fashion Corporate Responsibility Manual*, 55. Helsinki: Finnish Textile & Fashion.

GRI Standards

The GRI (www.globalreporting.org) was founded in 1997 by Ceres in Boston, Massachusetts, to develop a standardized sustainability reporting framework that would effectively capture and describe the sustainability activities that transpire in the economic, environmental, and social aspects of organizational operations.[34] The goal of the GRI has been to serve as a multi-stakeholder developed international independent organization that helps businesses, governments, and other organizations understand and communicate the impact of business on critical sustainability issues such as climate change, human rights, corruption, and many others. In so doing, reporting enterprises can make better decisions regarding the actions that should be taken toward a more sustainable economy and world. The Global Sustainability Standards Board (GSSB) issues and maintains the GRI reporting standards for organizations to use in their "sustainability reporting", described by the GSSB as "an organization's practice of reporting publicly on its economic, environmental, and/ or social impacts, and hence its contributions—positive or negative— towards the goal of sustainable development."[35]

When it was formed, the GRI was one of the pioneers of sustainability reporting. Since then, the GRI has been a primary driver of transforming sustainability reporting from a niche practice to one now adopted by a growing majority of organizations. The GRI's standards are the world's most widely used with respect to sustainability reporting and disclosure and are available for use by public agencies, firms and other organizations wishing to understand and communicate aspects of their economic, environmental, and social performance. The GRI's reporting standards are based on widely recognized international norms and normative frameworks on sustainability such as the UN Guiding Principles on Business

---

[34] Adapted from a description of the evolution of the Global Reporting Initiative included in Mink, K. 2012. "The Effects of Organizational Structure on Sustainability Report Compliance." Purdue University College of Technology Masters' Thesis. Available at http://docs.lib.purdue.edu/techmasters/62, 12–13.

[35] GRI 101: Foundation 2016. 2016. Amsterdam: Stichting Global Reporting Initiative.

and Human Rights, the ILO Conventions, the UN Global Compact Ten Principles, and the OECD Guidelines for Multinational Enterprises.

The latest version of the GRI's sustainability reporting framework, generally referred to as the "GRI Standards," were published, following extensive consultation, in October 2016 and formally went into effect for reports and other materials published on or after July 1, 2018. Reporting is required in three categories: economic (e.g., economic performance, indirect economic impacts, procurement practices etc.); environmental (e.g., materials, energy, water, transport, environmental grievance mechanisms etc.); and social, which includes labor practices and decent work (e.g., employment, occupational health and safety, training and education etc.), human rights (e.g., nondiscrimination, forced or compulsory labor, Indigenous rights etc.), society (e.g., local communities etc.) and product responsibility (e.g., customer health and safety, product and service labeling, customer privacy etc.). The GRI Standards include universal reporting principles, guidance on reporting contextual information about an organization and its sustainability reporting practices, and guidance on reporting how an organization manages a material reporting topic and each topic comes with its own specific requirements, recommendations, and guidance. The GRI is not a rating agency, does not monitor whether a particular organization has correctly applied its guidelines, and does not provide any certifications.

International Integrated Reporting Framework

The International Integrated Reporting Council (IIRC, www.theiirc.org) is a global coalition of regulators, investors, companies, standard setters, the accounting professionals, and NGOs dedicated to promoting communications about value creation as the next step in the evolution of corporate reporting.[36] The IIRC, which was founded in August 2010, released its International Integrated Reporting Framework in December 2013 as

---

[36] Carrots & Sticks: Global Trends in Sustainability Reporting Regulation and Policy (KPMG International, the Global Research Initiative ("GRI"), the United Nations Environment Programme ("UNEP") and the Centre for Corporate Governance in Africa, 2016), available at www.carrotsandsticks.net, 25.

a guide that companies could use to describe how their governance structure creates value in the short, medium, and long term; supports decision making that takes into account risks and includes mechanisms for addressing ethical issues; exceeds legal requirements; and ensures that the culture, ethics, and values of the company are reflected in its use of and effects on the company's "capitals" (described to include financial, manufactured, intellectual, human, social and relationship, and natural (i.e., the environment and natural resources) forms of value) and stakeholder relationships.[37]

The IRRC Framework was aimed primarily at producing information for long-term investors and providing companies with guiding principles and content elements that would govern the content of their integrated reports.[38] The executive summary to the framework explained that the drafters had taken a principles-based approach with the intent to strike an appropriate balance between flexibility and prescription that recognized the wide variation in individual circumstances of different organizations while enabling a sufficient degree of comparability across organizations to meet relevant information needs. According to the executive summary, the following guiding principles underpin the preparation of an integrated report, informing the content of the report and how information is presented[39]:

- *Strategic focus and future orientation*: An integrated report should provide insight into the organization's strategy, and how it relates to the organization's ability to create value in the short, medium, and long term, and to its use of and effects on the capitals
- *Connectivity of information*: An integrated report should show a holistic picture of the combination, interrelatedness and

---

[37] DeSimone, P. 2014. *Board Oversight of Sustainability Issues: A Study of the S&P 500*. IRRC Institute.

[38] The International <IR> Framework (International Integrated Reporting Council, December 2013).

[39] Id. at 5.

dependencies between the factors that affect the organization's ability to create value over time
- *Stakeholder relationships*: An integrated report should provide insight into the nature and quality of the organization's relationships with its key stakeholders, including how and to what extent the organization understands, takes into account and responds to their legitimate needs and interests
- *Materiality*: An integrated report should disclose information about matters that substantively affect the organization's ability to create value over the short, medium, and long term
- *Conciseness*: An integrated report should be concise
- *Reliability and completeness*: An integrated report should include all material matters, both positive and negative, in a balanced way and without material error
- *Consistency and comparability*: The information in an integrated report should be presented: (a) on a basis that is consistent over time; and (b) in a way that enables comparison with other organizations to the extent it is material to the organization's own ability to create value over time.

In addition, the executive summary to the framework explained that reports should include the following content elements, each of which are fundamentally linked to each other and are not mutually exclusive[40]:

- *Organizational overview and external environment*: What does the organization do and what are the circumstances under which it operates?
- *Governance*: How does the organization's governance structure support its ability to create value in the short, medium, and long term?
- *Business model*: What is the organization's business model?
- *Risks and opportunities*: What are the specific risks and opportunities that affect the organization's ability to create

---

[40] Id.

value over the short, medium, and long term, and how is the organization dealing with them?

- *Strategy and resource allocation*: Where does the organization want to go and how does it intend to get there?
- *Performance*: To what extent has the organization achieved its strategic objectives for the period and what are its outcomes in terms of effects on the capitals?
- *Outlook*: What challenges and uncertainties is the organization likely to encounter in pursuing its strategy, and what are the potential implications for its business model and future performance?
- *Basis of presentation*: How does the organization determine what matters to include in the integrated report and how are such matters quantified or evaluated?

Sustainability Accounting Standards Board

The Sustainability Accounting Standards Board (SASB) (www.sasb.org) is a US-based independent standards-setting organization for sustainability accounting standards that was incorporated in July 2011 to meet the needs of investors by fostering high-quality disclosure of material sustainability information. The SASB has established industry-based sustainability standards for the recognition and disclosure of material environmental, social, and governance impacts by companies traded on US exchanges.[41] The standards focus on known trends and uncertainties that are reasonably likely to affect the financial condition or operating performance of a company and therefore would be considered material under mandatory disclosure requirements, such as Regulation S-K applicable to disclosures made by US reporting companies in the public filings with the Securities and Exchange Commission (SEC). The SASB is an ANSI accredited

---

[41] Carrots & Sticks: Global Trends in Sustainability Reporting Regulation and Policy (KPMG International, the Global Research Initiative ("GRI"), the United Nations Environment Programme ("UNEP") and the Centre for Corporate Governance in Africa, 2016), available at www.carrotsandsticks.net, 25.

standards developer; however, it is not affiliated with FASB, GASB, IASB, or any other accounting standards board. SASB standards do not include a scoring system, instead the focus is on providing companies with a standardized methodology that can be deployed when reporting sustainability performance through their regular regulatory reporting to the SEC on Forms 10-K and 10-Q (i.e., an "integrated reporting" approach as opposed to separate non-financial reports). SASB's standards enable comparison of peer performance and benchmarking within an industry and the SASB has gathered the support of Bloomberg LP and the Rockefeller Foundation.

The SASB publishes the SASB Implementation Guide for Companies that provides the structure and the key considerations for companies seeking to implement sustainability accounting standards within their existing business functions and processes. The Guide helps companies to select sustainability topics; assess the current state of disclosure and management; embed SASB standards into financial reporting and management processes; support disclosure and management with internal control; and present information for disclosure. The SASB's online resource library also includes annual reports on the state of disclosure, industry briefs and standards and guidance on stakeholder engagement. Companies should monitor CSR disclosures by their peers and the SASB library has examples of disclosures made by companies in annual reports filed with the SEC on Forms 10-K, 8-K etc. Companies can also follow the reporting practices of competitors by reviewing sustainability reported registered with the GRI.

The SASB is involved in establishing industry standards for sustainability disclosure and reporting and has explained that the decision regarding whether a particular sustainability topic warrants an industry standard are made on the basis of several factors including the potential to affect corporate value, investor interest, relevance across an industry, actionability by companies (i.e., whether individual companies are in a position to control or influence actions with respect to a particular topic and whether there is consensus among companies and investors that a disclosure topic is reasonably likely to constitute material information for most companies in the industry). The SASB has established and currently maintains provisional sustainability accounting standards for 79 industries across 11 sectors and companies should refer to the standards applicable to their business operations to identify and understand the relevant disclosure topics.[42]

Report Formatting and Presentation

While the formatting and presentation of financial reporting has become somewhat standardized due to regulatory requirements, the development and maturation of professional financial accounting standards, and long-standing expectations of consumers of such information, there is no particular template in terms of format, length, and details that applies to sustainability reports and one can find a wide array of creative approaches to presenting information related to corporate sustainability and environmental and social impact. The persons responsible for preparing sustainability reports should seek out and review comparable reports prepared by peer companies in order to get a sense of how information might be presented and, not unimportantly, the ESG issues that peers have chosen to focus on and how they are describing and measuring progress on those issues.

While international standards like the GRI Standards provide a useful framework for comprehensive verification and reporting on environmental and social issues, companies should remember that it is important to tailor the information in their reports to the needs and expectations of their specific primary audiences. It has become more and more common among larger companies to generate large reports with glossy pictures, charts, and graphs and detailed breakdowns of data; however, many interested parties prefer to a short executive summary that highlights the most relevant information and provides links to detailed reports, case studies, and other materials. Information should be presented in a manner that reflects the company's overall organizational culture and provides recipients with a sense of what social responsibility means to the company's leaders and employees on a day-to-day basis. Finally, while reporting is

---

[42] See Sustainability Accounting Standards Board, Disclosure Topics Tables (July 11, 2017).

certainly a positive public relations tool and companies will be eager to showcase their impact-related successes, credibility demands that reports also include transparent assessments of areas in which the company may have failed to achieved its previously announced objectives and disclosures on the reasons for those failures and the steps the company is taking to improve its performance and the metrics that will be used to evaluate how well the remediation is proceeding.

About the Author

Alan S. Gutterman's prolific output of practical guidance and tools for legal and financial professionals, managers, entrepreneurs and investors has made him one of the best-selling individual authors in the global legal publishing marketplace. Alan has authored or edited over 90 books on sustainable entrepreneurship, leadership and management, business law and transactions, international law and business and technology management for a number of publishers. Alan has extensive experience as a partner and senior counsel with internationally recognized law firms counseling small and large business enterprises in the areas of general corporate and securities matters, venture capital, mergers and acquisitions, international law and transactions, strategic business alliances, technology transfers and intellectual property, and has also held senior management positions with several technology-based businesses. He received his A.B., M.B.A., and J.D. from the University of California at Berkeley, a D.B.A. from Golden Gate University, and a Ph. D. from the University of Cambridge. For more information about Alan and his activities, please visit his website at alangutterman.com.

Index

Note: Page numbers followed by "n" refers to notes.

OTHER TITLES IN THE FINANCE AND FINANCIAL MANAGEMENT COLLECTION

John Doukas, Old Dominion University, Editor

- *Small Business Finance and Valuation* by Rick Nason and Dan Nordqvist
- *Finance for Non-Finance Executives* by Anurag Singal
- *Blockchain Hurricane* by Kate Baucherel
- *Risk Management for Nonprofit Organizations* by Rick Nason and Omer Livvarcin
- *Understanding Behavioral BIA$* by Daniel C. Krawczyk and George H. Baxter
- *Conservative Options Trading* by Michael C. Thomsett
- *Valuation of Indian Life Insurance Companies* by Prasanna Rajesh
- *Understanding Momentum in Investment Technical Analysis* by Michael C. Thomsett
- *Escape from the Central Bank Trap, Second Edition* by Daniel Lacalle
- *The Art and Science of Financial Modeling* by Anurag Singal
- *Risk and Win!* by John Harvey Murray
- *Frontiers of Risk Management, Volume II* by Dennis Cox
- *Global Mergers and Acquisitions, Second Edition* by Abdol S. Soofi and Yuqin Zhang
- *Essentials of Enterprise Risk Management* by Rick Nason and Leslie Fleming
- *Essentials of Financial Risk Management* by Rick Nason and Brendan Chard
- *Frontiers of Risk Management, Volume I* by Dennis Cox
- *Numbers that Matter* by Evan Bulmer
- *Competing in Financial Markets* by Philip Cooper
- *Understanding Cryptocurrencies* by Arvind Matharu

Concise and Applied Business Books

The Collection listed above is one of 30 business subject collections that Business Expert Press has grown to make BEP a premiere publisher of print and digital books. Our concise and applied books are for...

- Professionals and Practitioners
- Faculty who adopt our books for courses
- Librarians who know that BEP's Digital Libraries are a unique way to offer students ebooks to download, not restricted with any digital rights management
- Executive Training Course Leaders
- Business Seminar Organizers

Business Expert Press books are for anyone who needs to dig deeper on business ideas, goals, and solutions to everyday problems. Whether one print book, one ebook, or buying a digital library of 110 ebooks, we remain the affordable and smart way to be business smart. For more information, please visit www.businessexpertpress.com, or contact sales@businessexpertpress.com.

www.ingramcontent.com/pod-product-compliance
Lightning Source LLC
Chambersburg PA
CBHW061210220326
41599CB00025B/4588